How *I'm Already Home* (edition one) has helped others...

"I wish I had this book at the beginning of my marriage to a soldier. It would have made the many deployments a much different experience. I think as military wives, we need to use all the tools available to help us cope with our special circumstances."

— M. Fichtner, the forever loyal wife of a Special Forces soldier

"You're doing a great thing with this book. I, along with hundreds of thousands, thank you for bringing light to this lifestyle. It is nothing glamorous, but it is most rewarding in the end. I appreciate your work and devotion!"

— OS1 Timothy Mollock, USN

"In skimming through part of the book, some of the things in it brought me to tears. There were some of your wonderful ideas that I'd like to employ with my own children since their dad has recently been gone a lot more on business trips. Thank you for taking the time to do this ministry!"

— Charlene Johnson (via email)

"Today the reality of how much your book has helped hit when a lady emailed me (I am Coordinator of our family support group) asking for help with her children whose daddy is deployed in Iraq now. All the ideas that I gave her came from your book! What joy it was to pass along quality information that worked wonders in our home."

— Jeannette (via email)

"My sister discovered your book and ordered a copy for me. My husband has now deployed for the second time in less that two years. He is now in Iraq. My sincerest thanks to you for putting together such a wonderful and inspirational resource. Your ideas help ease some of the loneliness for me."
— Kelly Ayala (via email)

"What a heart-touching book. I am amazed at the creativity and compassion exhibited in these examples! Makes me want to do something special for my kids tonight."
— Laura Benjamin, 7 yr Veteran of the US Air Force (enlisted)

"The Flat Daddy is an awesome idea. I loved that one! We actually used a lot of the ideas. I have my wives do what you called the "Legacy Letters." That way they are writing a little over time and they have something to send, even when they think they have nothing to say. Thank you again."
— Angel Hernandez, Marine wife (3dAABn Bravo K.V.)

"After reading your book, it became obvious to me that several of my men's wives must have used your tips while we were deployed in Afghanistan. These guys always had a smile on their faces and were the envy of the base. Thanks for making our stay overseas that much more bearable!"
— CPT Diggs Brown, USSF, author of *Your Neighbor Went to War*

"Your book is absolutely wonderful! As you can see, I am all over it. This is indeed one for Oprah!"
— V. Palmer, New Jersey (via email)

"Thank you especially for writing a book to help our military men and women and their families stay connected with each other during deployment."
— First Lady, Laura Bush

"...grass-roots success story...a welcome tonic for families missing their loved ones."
— *Ladies Home Journal*, October 2004

"As a military spouse one is never alone. There are countless sources of aid and guidance available. *I'm Already Home* is one of the most creative and comprehensive."
— Captain Gerald Coffee, US Navy (Ret.)
P.O.W. North Vietnam, 7 years

"I cannot say enough about wonderful people like you who have insight to the military life and know how much it means to us that the American people care. You hear so much about the negative side and it's nice to know, hear, and see someone non-military who is involved to support the troops and their families."
— Jo Ann Cherry, Alabama FRG and military wife

"I wholeheartedly endorse the book and the many ways, so simple, that anyone can use those great ideas to just put that smile on the face of their loved one, at perhaps just the right moment. It gives them hope, happiness, and knowledge that their relationship is so vital."
— Janet Weber, MSG MIARNG

"This little book of tips on staying connected has become an important part of the lives of many military families with parents who have been deployed."
— *Rocky Mountain News*, May 31, 2004

"I got great tips from your book and I feel you are really touching a lot of lives and making a difference. Dealing with deployment is without a doubt the toughest thing I have ever faced in my life. I can't help but think of the families that are going to be in my shoes. Be persistent as there are a lot of families that are really going to need this book."

— Angela Orn, military spouse

I'm Already Home...
Again

Keeping your family close
while on assignment or deployment

Expanded 2nd Edition

Elaine Gray Dumler

ᬵ

Published by Frankly Speaking
6460 W. 98th Court, Westminster, CO 80021 • 303-430-0592
Elaine@ElaineDumler.com

ᬵ

Visit www.ImAlreadyHome.com

ᬵ

I'm Already Home...Again – Keeping your family close
while on assignment or deployment
Elaine Gray Dumler
ISBN 978-0-9740359-1-8

Printed in the United States of America
BA   10 9 8 7 6 5 4 3 2 1
Library of Congress Control Number: 2006900684

About the Cover

The photograph sitting on the desk is by U.S. Air Force SSgt. Thomas J. Sobczyk, Jr. and is used with permission of both the photographer and the wonderful family portrayed in the picture. Meet the Hoffmanns: Lt Col Pete Hoffmann is from the Wisconsin Air National Guard's 128th Air Refueling Wing, and is embracing his family upon his return from Operation Enduring Freedom on May 1, 2002. Shown in the photo are his wife, Sue Hoffmann, and their 12-year-old twin daughters, Kassey and Trina. Not shown, because she's lovingly engulfed in the middle of the hug, is 10-year-old Rachel.

Cover design and layout by:
Karen Saunders, MacGraphics
Aurora, Colorado

Cover photo taken by:
Joyce Jay
303-420-8533

Edited by:
Denise Hmieleski
P.O. Box 709
Lafayette, CO 80026-0709

Page layout by:
Laura Vincent, BOSS Printing
Broomfield, Colorado

Acknowledgements

I am grateful to many people who helped with this book. Thanks to LeAnne Ahern, Colorado National Guard Family Readiness Specialist who provided information and proofreading resources. Laura Benjamin, Management Development Consultant/Speaker/Author and seven-year Veteran of the United States Air Force (enlisted), thanks for reading the manuscript for military accuracy and for all your kind words along the way. You always told me I was on the right track. Immense gratitude goes to Major Ann Dirks, originally with the Colorado National Guard Family Programs Office for spending so much time with me in interviews, and for supporting the distribution of the book to families. You helped me to put a "face" on all the military contacts I made.

I can never repay Denise Hmieleski for the amazing editing job. You made my words actually sound like I wanted them to!

Thank you to the members of my Mastermind group: Fred Berns, Sarah Michel, Jay Arthur, Brad Montgomery, and LeAnn Thieman. You all remained faithful cheerleaders and are more important to me than you know. Thanks to Cyndi Manuel and Mary Fichtner for the many hours of research, verifying, and phone work that you devoted to the project.

Special thanks goes out to Lisa White, unit volunteer for the Colorado Army National Guard's Family Readiness Center for spending all that time on the phone with me. Your insights and ideas fueled me to expand the book to cover more areas. Special thanks to Julie-ann Goldstein, Cindy Bruschwein, Debi Geisler and the hundreds of other amazing military spouses for sharing your families with me and making me feel like I was invited into your living rooms. I thank all the wonderful volunteers at Family Readiness and Support Centers for all the work they do and for being the vehicles for getting this book into the hands of the families it can help.

Finally, I thank God for planting the original vision of the book in my heart and selecting me to be the messenger for helping to make better families.

Dedication

This book is dedicated to my husband (Larry) and
my son (Bryan) who showed me how rewarding
it is to raise kids.
And to my parents (Ralph and Josie),
sisters (Rondi and Nancy), and brother (Brad)
where I learned about love and laughter
from the beginning—even in the tough times.

Beyond the dedication, this book
wouldn't have been written without the
emotional inspiration that came from
my sister (Nancy Early) and her
wonderful family (Jim, Stacy and Kenny).
When Nancy lost her battle with cancer,
her family showed more love and support
than I thought was possible.
They were also an inspiration to many
who were around them during that time.
I love you.

Table of Contents

"Freedom is Not Free"
by Jacena LouEllen Winburn 1

Welcome 3

Chapter 1 –
Ideas for the Pre-deployment Phase 9

    Leaving a Piece of You Behind 11

    Smile – You Should be in Pictures! 18

    You're My Top Priority 23

    A Conversation with Lisa White –
    NG Youth Volunteer 26

Chapter 2 –
Ideas for the Deployment Phase 33

    Thinking of You 34

    Because I Understand 37

    For Better or Worse –
    Spouses...Are You Listening? 40

    Let's Get Personal 48

    It's All About Communication 50

    Fun Projects to Get the Kids Involved 55

    More Fun Stuff and Projects 59

        Special Ideas for Younger Children
        (under 10) 65

        Special Ideas for Older Children and Teens
        (over 10) 67

    "Innocence" *by Molly Waneka* 71

    Pets and Deployment 73

Ideas for Extended Family Members 78

How Communities, Co-workers, Churches,
Schools and Neighbors can Help 82

    Schools Are on Your Side 91

    Spiritual Protection 97

"Happy Birthday!" and "Happy Holidays!"–
Celebrations Across the Miles 101

Chapter 3 –
About Family Services Centers 105

Chapter 4 –
Post-deployment... and Beyond
Reunion and Reintegration 113

    It All Starts at the Airport 116

    Fitting Back in Again 119

    Reunion: Prospect and Possibility
    by Linda Engelman 124

Returning to Single Life 127

Epilogue 131

Resources & Support 133

In Appreciation 143

Permissions & Information 145

Footnotes 146

About the Author 147

Also By Elaine Dumler 149

Ordering Information 151

Freedom is Not Free
by Jacena LouEllen Winburn

Freedom is not now, nor has it ever been free;
just look at what it's costing someone even as young as me.
The Army has taken my daddy away to that distant land,
to fight for America and to make a democratic stand.

He was not here to put up our Christmas tree.
In March, my eighteenth birthday will be very lonely.
When April rolls around, he misses my first and only Senior Prom.
We'll mail him the thousands of pictures
that will be taken by my mom.

Summer and May, at High school graduation, it's all up to me.
Then on to August, my first day of college, and where is he?
Freedom is not free.
The price is the absence of my daddy.

"Cowgirl up," is one of the things he would say,
"don't let those tears get in your way.
I love and I approve of you –
and I want you to be proud of me, too!

"You've got to stand for something,
because someday, it will mean everything.
Practice what you preach.
Live what you teach.

"Who you are shows in where you go.
What you are shows in how you get there, so –
mind your manners, live a full life and love God.
Always be aware of the path that you trod."

The worry, sadness and pain in my mother's eyes,
show even when she doesn't let us see her cry.
"Head up – chin out,
God, duty and country IS what it's all about."

We struggle to get by without him each and every day.
Don't believe it – it doesn't get any easier, by the way.
The flagpole in our yard holds the symbol of this great country.
Sometimes it just reminds me that Daddy's not here with me.

But, I'll always love the strength in my daddy's hands.
He taught me to be patriotic, to volunteer,
and what it means to be a true American.
It's not how much money you have, or status quo,
it's answering the call, when asked to go.

He raised his hand and said, "Here am I, send me."
No, to me, Freedom never has been and never will be "Free."
The cost, I must willingly and without regret, gladly pay –
because, I am my father's daughter today and every day.

Jaceena won the 2005 Essay Contest as a high school senior in Kentucky, with her poem "Freedom is Not Free." She is the daughter of MSG John Geisler and his wife, Debi. At this writing, MSG Geisler is deployed to Iraq.

Welcome

If you've picked up this book, it's probably because you are personally affected by a military separation. Maybe you are a soldier about to be deployed. You've heard from the Family Readiness Center that you need to stay in touch with your family, and now you want to know how. Or maybe you're a family member of someone who's being deployed or on active duty training. The military doesn't enlist only soldiers, airmen, sailors and marines; they enlist families. You're looking for ways to lessen the impact of the separation.

That's what this book is about. It's about you. It's about your family. It's about keeping you close when you're apart. Togetherness—it's the heart of the family; it's the heart of your family.

For those of you new to *I'm Already Home...Again,* you are reading the second edition of the book that's been updated and expanded to better meet the needs of families. Over the past two years, I have had the privilege of meeting and talking with thousands of military family members.

You shared so many original and wonderful ideas about how you're staying connected that it was time to give 195 all new ideas and resources back to you. Also, times have changed. It was appropriate to expand the sections on returning home and family reintegration, address redeployment, and create chapters about ways your co-workers, extended families and communities can stay involved with you. I learned that pets suffer separation anxiety, too, so I didn't forget them either.

Don't worry, you'll still find 79 of your old favorites from the first edition like "Flat Daddy," the exchange of hand drawings, talking picture frame, and a conversation with Lisa White. Your resource section is updated and expanded with three times as many helpful websites that have been sent to me to pass along.

I define a family as a particular group of people who love, care for, and support each other. Family can also be considered a place. It's a place where you should feel safe and cared about even if other family members don't always agree with you. The family is a foundation for your social and emotional growth, financial stability, and education. You carry what you absorb from its teaching as you take your place in society. Families may look very different these days, but hopefully, they contain the same kind of love.

American families are being challenged by trying times in the current political life of our country. When war or the threat of war begins to infiltrate our nation, we have lots of moms, dads, sons, and daughters in the military waiting for deployment or extended assignments. This causes families to be separated for incredibly long spans of time and by phenomenal distances. Many spouses remain at home to handle the roles previously held by both, and the kids may be left to hear bedtime stories from others for a while.

No matter where we are, we need to remember that distance is just an illusion. When we take the time to stay connected, we can still feel close to someone who's thousands of miles away. If we don't take the time, we can feel distanced from someone who is at the other end of the house.

As someone who has many friends serving in the military, I understand the difficulty of being separated from one's family. I didn't grow up in a military family, but I don't think that's a requirement to be able to feel the impact that being in the military has on a family. Before I met him, my husband Larry served in the Army National Guard from 1969–1975. I was a carefree student in the late '60s and have two vivid recollections of the war in Vietnam. The first was when a friend of mine lost her brother; the second was when I watched a group of college fraternity brothers sit in silence in front of the television watching the draft lottery on December 1, 1969. I swear that was the only time I ever saw college kids so quiet. I remember feeling very lucky not to have close family members in the age range to serve.

During the conflict in the Persian Gulf, my own son was only eight. Things are different now. My son is 22, and I realize how close I am to being the mom of someone who could be in the military. Because of the tragic events of September 11, 2001, the United States will always be on alert for the threat of terrorism. At all times, we have over 60,000 troops stationed around the world on assignment to fight terrorism.

The faces of the brave people who serve in our armed forces have changed, too. In the Vietnam War, an overwhelming majority of U.S. service men and women were single. Today, 57% are married, and of those, 46% have children. 73% of those children are 11 years of age or younger. The biggest changes, however, have occurred for women. 14% of the military population are now women, and 20% of these women are in joint service marriages where both spouses are serving.[1]

During the Gulf War we became even more aware that mothers, along with fathers, were being deployed. So, in addition to more frequent deployments, family separations are having a greater impact. It's no wonder that in a U.S. Army Medical Research report, 59% of soldiers stated that the number of deployments had hurt the stability of their marriage and put a strain on their families.[2]

The Department of Defense has responded to this need. They are working hard to provide support for its military families through the creation of Family Centers all around the world. These centers offer youth programs at a total of 320 locations to serve the 1.3 million children of military families.[3]

Family separations are occurring more frequently than ever before, and that's why this book is so timely. The ideas presented here are simple steps you can take to keep you and your loved ones as connected as possible. You'll see what other people do to bridge the distance, and I'll also be sharing some stories from my own life and family about keeping that strong connection. Some are funny and some are touching; I hope all will be inspiring.

I've interviewed over 600 military families, done personal research, and compiled the observations and ideas within these pages. While some strategies are specific to military personnel, others are tailored to the unique demands of the military family. Included are things your family can do before, during, and after deployment. Remember, most of these ideas are directly from you...what's worked for you in the past.

Technology has certainly helped close the gap between us when we're apart, but it doesn't replace the special times, the special moments, and the personal ways you have of sharing time with the family when you're right there with each other. This book will help you take your own special, personal times with you when you're away.

I'm Already Home...Again is designed to help you discover unique and wonderful ways to stay connected when you're apart from each other. It's as simple as that. You may already have a couple of traditions in place but would just like to try something new for a change. I hope you find at least a few new ideas that spark you to think, "That's cool. We should try that." Take an idea and apply a special twist to it so that *your* family can own it now.

Throughout the book I refer to soldiers, airmen, sailors and marines as they relate to where a particular idea originated from and who submitted it. Please know that I mean no disrespect when I use these references interchangeably. You're all part of our collective "military family."

I encourage you to write on the pages and make personal notes in the margins when something strikes you. Then you'll know where to quickly find that special idea.

My prayer is for every serviceperson's safe return, and I hope that the messages in *I'm Already Home...Again* will play a small part in easing your family through the challenging experience of remote assignments and deployments.

Savor your family like you savor a fine wine.
Take the time to truly experience
ALL the benefits they have to offer.
Don't gulp them; just sip slowly.

Chapter 1

Ideas for the Pre-deployment Phase
(from 6 to 8 weeks before deployment)

One of the most difficult challenges for family members of those who are deployed is that our hearts ache for the safety of our loved one. The uncertainty of his/her return is always hanging over our heads, and we just can't seem to let it go.

I was scared when my son, Bryan, got behind the wheel of a car for the first time. I was scared when he went off to college. How could I possibly take care of him? I couldn't. I had to let him go. A friend gave me a verse that helped me through the challenging times of letting my son grow up. This verse has been on my refrigerator since his 16th birthday. Although it's more about "letting go" in the natural course of growing up, I pass it along to you with my wish that it will make your separation easier and help you with some of that worry:

As parents and grandparents, uncles and aunts, one of the hardest things we may have to do is let go of our children so that they can learn something new. So whether we are handing over the car keys to a newly licensed driver or taking the training wheels off a bike for a first-grader, we may hesitate or feel unsure that what we are doing is right.

But we do more than let go of the car keys and take off the training wheels to allow the children to experience learning firsthand. We also pray for them, remaining strong and supportive, for we know that God is taking greater care of them than we could ever hope to.

Letting go and letting God be in charge, we are able to relax and enjoy the experience of watching our children— and even adults—discover more about what they are capable of doing and achieving.

Reprinted with permission from *Daily Word*™

Let's get started on our journey...

Leaving a Piece of You Behind

It's interesting where ideas originate. Many times we only have to look to what we do in the course of our daily lives. This first connection idea was contributed by a single working mom and her 11-year-old daughter. Eleven is a tough age for any child and can be just as hard on parents when they can't be around as much as they'd like. This was the case in their particular family.

1 Every morning Mom would see Ashley off to school and then follow her out the door on the way to work. Mom worked a long day and often didn't arrive home until 6:00 or 6:30. Ashley would come home after school with all her social crises and just want to know that her mom was available, but the house was empty. Mom also felt a huge void during her workday as she longed to be home so she could listen. *How can I let Ashley know that even when we're not in the same room, we can still feel the touch of each other's hands and heart?* That thought gave way to an idea.

After dinner that evening, Mom got two sheets of copy paper and a set of colorful crayons. Then she parked her daughter at the kitchen table. "We're going to color!" her mom replied to the look of surprise on Ashley's face. Then she instructed Ashley to set her hand flat on the paper, take a crayon and trace around it just like she used to do in kindergarten, and she would do the same thing on her own paper.

When she had done that, Ashley looked up and said, "Ok, now what?"

11

"Now we're going to color together," replied her mom. "Pick up your favorite colors and have fun coloring in your hand. Be as creative as you'd like. Make it look like 'you,' and I'll do it, too."

So both of them spent 15 minutes completing their works of art. When they were done, they held them next to each other with a glow of personal satisfaction.

Then to Ashley's surprise, her mom said, "Ok, now we switch them! You give me yours and I'll give you mine."

Each drawing was slipped into a plastic page protector to keep it clean, and then exchanged with the following instructions from Ashley's mom: "We each have a small piece of each other. Ashley, you put my picture in one of your notebooks, and I'll hang your picture next to my desk. Whenever you wish that I were there with you to listen or reassure you, open your notebook and place your hand on the drawing of my hand. In that instant, no matter where you are, we'll be together. When I'm at work and get homesick for you, I'll place my hand over yours on the drawing by my desk. I know I'll feel your love and thoughts coming through the drawing. When we have each other's hands, we have each other's hearts. No matter what, we'll always be together."

What a wonderful way to realize that distance is relative. The people you love, and who love you, are the most important people in your life. When children grow up, they'll realize that you weren't always together, but they will remember the creative ways you chose to stay in touch with them while you were gone. Spend some time with the members of your family to create your own *handprints*. When you're thousands of miles apart, just touch the handprints and you'll be transported home in your mind.

A few months after the first edition of *I'm Already Home* was released I received an envelope in the mail. It was from a soldier who had been stationed in Iraq and was now safely home. In the envelope was a well-worn folded piece of paper. When I unfolded it, a few errant grains of sand fell to the floor. It was the hand drawing his daughter had made and sent to him in Iraq. He told me that he kept it folded in the pocket of his fatigues. He often took it out, unfolded it and placed his hand over the hand drawing. It helped with the loneliness.

2 Here's what one woman wrote to me in an email, so you can see that the hand drawing idea can apply anytime during deployment. "My favorite idea out of the book was the handprint idea. My husband was already gone when we found this book, so our children and daddy could not sit down and do the drawings together. But my husband carried the hand print that my daughter mailed to him at all times. She made him two and he hung one up in his quarters as well."

3 I'm amazed at how far the hand drawing ideas can go and what an impact that has. Billie writes: "My son and I use your 'hand drawing' idea but use the 10 fingers. I came up with this because my 4 year old son tells me to count to 10 when I miss him. So I use the 10 fingers to 'count off' 10 reasons we love and miss each other."

How about this variation: Outline your hands in a light pencil. Then take a black pen or fine line marker and outline over the pencil with tiny printed words from scriptures or personal messages.

4 Let's ask a serious question: Can you sing? Even if you don't have a voice like Frank Sinatra or Whitney Houston, your kids will love hearing it. Record a "sing-along" tape or CD for the kids to play in the car. They can sing their favorite songs along with you, or they can just listen to their favorite recording artist— YOU!

5 Do you have favorite stories that you like to read to your children at bedtime? They don't have to miss out on hearing them. Videotape yourself reading bedtime stories for your children. They can play the tape and read along with you. Do you have a new baby? Videotape yourself singing lullabies.

6 Have your airman put his or her picture on a coffee mug or drinking glass for each member of the family. Then you can all have morning coffee (or juice) together.

7 Change your computer screensaver and/or wallpaper to a fun message from you; or how about a special photo of you or your family?

8 This idea comes to you from my son, Bryan. "Ever since I've been in kindergarten, Mom had a saying she told me every morning when I left for school. She'd say, 'I love you with my whole life. Have a great day.' Then I turned 16, and she added, 'Drive carefully.' When Mom traveled, I missed hearing it when I walked out the door. She bought a small portable picture frame where you can record a 10-second voice message. She put a picture of the two of us in one side and recorded what she  always told me so that I could play it whenever she was on the road. I took it with me to college. She could send me off to classes in the same way she did all through school."

P.S. Over the past two years this has become one of the most popular ideas. Record the kids saying "Good Morning, Daddy" or "Good Morning, Mommy" and send it to where they are on assignment for a wonderful awakening every morning. Or consider recording your serviceperson's voice before he/she leaves to wake the family at home. I know these picture frames are all over the world!

9 Have the kids make a collage that you can take with you. If that's not possible, then you make one about yourself to leave at home. You'll need the following supplies:

- Glue
- Piece of construction paper
- Scissors

- Old magazines or catalogs
- Crayons, pens, or colored pencils

Cut out pictures of things you like and things you like to do, such as fishing, biking, reading, soccer, basketball, and examples of your favorite colors, clothes, movies, cartoon characters, etc. It's your personality. Glue the pictures onto the construction paper in whatever way you want—the crazier the better. Let dry and laminate it or put it in a page protector.

10 I love the fun of this idea shared by a wife/mother. I know it will make you smile and want to come up with your own special "good-bye routine." Thanks for letting me share this.

"My husband has a good-bye routine that he's done with our daughter ever since she was born. He kisses her forehead, her nose, both eyes, her cheeks, her chin, then they smooch. My daughter is a year and a half old now and she really enjoys her good-bye time with Daddy, especially since she knows what to expect and can participate more; i.e., turning her cheek to face him. She usually ends up in a fit of giggles afterward."

11 Because it was a 12-month deployment "boots on ground," a deck of 52 playing cards was given to our soldier. As a countdown to returning, he mails home one card a week (hopefully with a letter) and he started when his boots hit foreign soil.

12 Our area received Teddy Bears from an organization called "Bear Cares." The bears wore a tee-shirt with a pocket to hold a note from a serviceperson (written before he/she leaves) to their loved ones. This way family members can hug the bear and read the note.

A memory is a photograph taken by the heart.

Smile – You Should be in Pictures!

When we think of staying in touch, we usually think of using photographs. Digital cameras are great for taking pictures "on the spot" and emailing them right away. Here are great tactics for sharing pictures:

13 You can make your favorite photos into fabric transfers. Put a fabric photo onto tee shirts, hats, or even pillowcases for your kids. They'd love to "wear" a picture of the two of you. Many families made pillowcases with family photos on them and sent them to their serviceperson about three weeks after they were deployed. It's a nice surprise.

14 A friend of mine who travels a lot selected six of his favorite photos, scanned them, and printed them onto two sheets of photo paper. He placed them back-to-back in a plastic page protector. It's easier to tuck that page away and have six to eight photos all together. One deployed mom slept with her family photos in her pillowcase.

15 Go to a local copy shop, Office Depot®, or other office supply store that provides a copy service, and create a calendar with a family photo for each month. Then you can use this calendar at home to mark off the days until your serviceperson returns. Make a second calendar and send it with your serviceperson. Then they can count down the days just like at home.

16 Take a child's school picture and make a refrigerator magnet out of it. The easy way is to buy a magnetic plastic frame and glue little jewels and rhinestones on it or decorate it with paint pens.

17 Here's a contribution from a ninth grade girl: "I keep pictures of my dad while he's away on trips or when I'm just not close to him." This comment makes me think that we, as parents, often carry photos of our children, but how many of our children have been given pictures of *us* to have with them? You can take care of that right now.

18 "At a family wedding or other holiday where friends are together, take lots of pictures. Then have everyone write personal notes on 4" X 6" note cards (same size as the photos). Put the pictures and notes into an album—nothing fancy, just a little "slip in" album from Wal-Mart™."

19 I like it when I come across a good idea that also doesn't cost much! "My daughter takes the bus to school. I made a card with her bus information, my phone number, etc. on one side and on the flip side put a picture of her with her daddy. I laminated it (with a luggage-tag-sized piece of laminate from Kinkos™), put a key ring on it, and clipped it to her backpack. Now anytime she misses her dad she can peek in there and see the two of them together. Cost: $1.29."

20 Have pictures of the deployed parent everywhere—including the child's bedroom. Hang one right over the head of his/her bed and say "Now Daddy is watching over you always" or something like that.

21 This idea may not be applicable to all area assignments, but where it is, it's a good one. "I made a curtain to enclose my husband's bunk. It was created to work like a shower curtain. Stitched on the inside of the curtain toward his bed were all of our family pictures so we were always with him before he went to bed." The photos were printed from the home computer onto t-shirt transfer paper, cut out, ironed onto the curtain fabric, and stitched in place.

22 Give your school-age child a disposable camera and have him/her take pictures of weekday or weekend activities. The more fun the better. Others can help by taking pictures of him/her in class, playing a sport, etc. Have the photos developed and send them in the order in which they were taken—to be a part of "A day in the life of...."

23 Cindy Bruschwein and her 4-year-old daughter, Sarah, introduce you to *Flat Daddy*. Three months after Dave Bruschwein was deployed, Cindy took a "waist up" photo of him (dressed in fatigues) to a local print shop. They enlarged it to life size and mounted it on foam board—like a big, two-dimensional paper doll. "He was missing so many family gatherings," said Cindy. *Flat Daddy* then traveled to graduations, weddings, and other celebrations where he took his rightful place in the photographs. Copies were sent to Dave overseas so he could see where he'd been while he was gone! Cindy keeps an album at home of everywhere *Flat Daddy* has been...even tucking Sarah into bed. This was actually the real reason that *Flat Daddy* was created—to give Sarah a daily

visual reminder of Dave so that she'd recognize him when he returned from Iraq after 15 months. Sarah had just turned one year old when he left. Speaking of Sarah, when he was deployed, the real Dave received a *Flat Sarah*, minus the foam board, so he could see how much she'd grown.

24 Those of you who have heard me present at your family readiness conference know how this idea has taken off! In many families, *Flat Daddy* has held watch over Halloween candy and visited Chuck E. Cheese™. Here's something another family did as a variation to *Flat Daddy*: "Going off your *Flat Daddy* idea we kind of did the reverse on a smaller scale. I laminated wallet size photos of the kids for my husband to take with him, and now he's sending pictures of himself by icebergs (he's in Greenland) holding up the pictures of Kelsi and David, so they feel like they are there with him. My son asks him now,

'Where have we gone together, Daddy?' and my husband can tell them where he's toted them along to."

25 Based on *Flat Daddy*, one woman gave birth to their daughter while her husband was at sea. "When your little one is born, take a full length picture (which I'm sure you will) and have it printed in FULL SIZE (21" long or however long he/she is when born). Then cut out around the edges of the figure. Fold this photo and mail it to your husband. He'll have the real feeling of experiencing exactly how big his new child is in his arms. It works like a dream, and he'll have the best looking 'pin up' on the ship."

A friend of mine saw *Flat Daddy* and came up with this little slogan that he thought would fit:

> *"Just a little me,*
> *a uniformed clone.*
> *I'm not far away,*
> *I'm Already Home!"*
>
> — ©2005 Michael Craig Daniels

You're My Top Priority

Sometimes it's just enough to do something that says, "You're my top priority." It's a reminder of how important it can be to your family to know that they are always on the top of your mind.

I read that actors Kevin Bacon and Kyra Sedgwick take special care to keep their family close. Whenever possible, Kevin gets up with his kids every morning to take them to school. He's involved in every detail of their lives. With both actors working, it's sometimes a challenge to make time together, so he has instituted a "two week rule" where the family never goes longer than two weeks without all getting together. I also read that Kevin values the time he spends with his kids so much that he won't give out autographs when he's with them because at that moment they are his top priority.

26 When my son comes home from college for the holidays, there comes a time when he has to return. When Bryan is packing, I go up and sit on his bed just to be there with him. I don't get in the way or try to do anything other than what he specifically asks me to do. I just want to enjoy him one more time before he leaves. You can do the same thing. Spend some time with the person who is leaving by helping him/her pack; but understand that this is an emotional time for everyone, so don't get in the way. It will give you some "alone" time to talk.

27 This is especially good when Mom is the "doctor" around the house and she is the one who's gone: Assemble a *Cuts and Scrapes Box* that includes antiseptic, Band-aids® in colors or cartoon characters, a lollypop, and a card with a "Kiss" made with lipstick from you to make it all better.

28 Make copies of basic, simple line drawings from clip art programs, and print them onto one side of white paper. Then put them together to make a coloring book. For additional pages, have a cartoonist make a caricature of each family member (don't forget the family pets) and have these added to the book. You can have a copy center bind it with a comb binding so that it lays flat. Leave the book with your child along with a special box of crayons.

29 Order a subscription to your children's favorite magazine (they have them for all ages) and have it come each month while you're away. They'll think of you every time they read it.

30 Make a personalized rubber stamp that has your child's name on it. He or she can use it to personally stamp every letter written to you.

Here are a couple of ideas about notes:

31 Head out to the store and pick up a bunch of small greeting cards. Both American Greetings® and Hallmark® have at least one series of 99¢ cards—

so go crazy. They're small (only about the size of a playing card) so they're perfect for leaving in drawers, purses, shoes, or medicine cabinets just as reminders that "you're my top priority." Hide these cards before you leave so that they're found at different times during your assignment.

32 In addition to the cards, here's something even easier. Before you head out the door, write some special notes on separate small slips of paper. Try writing them on colored construction paper or funny Post-it® notes, too. This is especially great for younger kids because the notes stand out better. Now go around the house and tape these "good morning" notes and sayings on places where they'll be noticed first thing in the morning. Tape them on the inside of the front door, the bathroom mirror, on the car's steering wheel, the coffee maker, and in the refrigerator.

You can prepare some notes and cards ahead of time and leave them with the spouse or caregiver who is remaining home. Have them hide them, or give them out at important times or events that happen in the lives of your family while you're away.

So you think hiding fun notes and personal sayings are only for the kids? Think again. Here's what a deployed soldier wrote to me: "When I was sent to Iraq for a good while, whenever I would unpack something I would find each note. To this day, and even though I'm 40 years old, I still love getting those little notes."

A Conversation with Lisa White

I had the privilege of talking with Lisa White, the youth volunteer for the Colorado Army National Guard's Family Readiness Center. This center is a support agency for deployed soldiers and their families. She is paramount in establishing a youth camp for kids so they can be in an environment with other kids who are experiencing just what they are going through.

As a volunteer, Lisa has gotten together with many husbands and wives to talk about how to stay connected with everyone when one or both parents are deployed. She strives for face-to-face meetings because it allows her to get to know the families she is working with. This lets her learn about their lifestyle so she can customize connection ideas for that family. And customize she does! The most important tip she gives is the importance of *planning ahead*. You can now benefit from some of the wonderful ideas and thoughts that Lisa cared enough to share with us. Enjoy!

33 This idea works well for older boys: Often when Dad is deployed, boys feel like they're the "man of the house" now. The problem is, this often puts too much pressure on them. They feel like they have to take on extra responsibilities, when instead, they need to stay little boys. Lisa's suggestion to help waylay that pressure, but still understand that the feelings of responsibility are important, is to make up a list of what the son can specifically do to be a part of helping the household to run efficiently. This list can include:

- Take out the garbage.
- Get the newspaper every morning.
- Sit next to Mom at the dinner table.
- Answer the front door when someone arrives.

Little kids can take on roles, too, but be sure to make the list together. The big thing is to pre-plan and have open communication. You can set up the same type of list for girls, especially if Mom is deployed.

34 When the wife or husband goes away, there are many emotions that take place at home. This can be confusing for some children, and they're not sure how they should respond. Since kids like lists, make a list of emotions they're bound to feel or observe, and how they might react. Then they'll know what to do. This might look like:

If Mommy feels like this ___(sad)___, or does this ___(cry)___, then you can do this ___(give her a hug)___ for me, or tell her this ___("I'm glad you're my mom")___ .

You can do the same for older kids who often want to deal with their feelings on their own. It's like they're really saying, "Just sit here, hug me, acknowledge me, but leave me alone." This works best for when dads go away because it clears the emotions.

"When someone leaves," Lisa says, "it's not just about pictures and notes. It's about everyday life."

The most important thing to remember in the pre-deployment stage is to prepare ahead of time. Be aware of how the normal workings of the household schedule are going to be upset. By thinking of this first, you'll be able to cover for the voids that will be left.

35 Begin by being aware of the traditions that will change. What if it's a tradition for Dad to take his daughter out for breakfast on her birthday? What happens if he's gone over that birthday? Or if Mom makes it a Friday afternoon tradition to bring home a specific candy bar to her nine-year-old son, and then she ships out? By writing these down and being aware of them, the remaining parent can carry on the tradition. Now Dad at home can bring home the candy bars, or Mom at home can make the birthday breakfast reservations. By recording everything, it makes it a lot easier on the parent left at home. Some other things to write down:

- How the laundry gets done.
- Mom's and/or Dad's everyday chores.
- Standard shopping lists for what you buy every week.
- Favorite recipes or dishes. (Ask a neighbor or close friend to have your family's favorite food made and brought over once a week. People like to help.)

36 Strategies that *count down* the time apart help to keep it in perspective. If you know you'll be gone for a long time, write a quick note once a week for your children. Either leave these notes at home with a caregiver to be given out personally, or mail one each Monday—especially if you'll be missing a milestone event.

37 For small children (two to four years old), make a placemat for them. Use drawings, photos of you together, sayings, stickers, or just colored shapes. Make it together and take it to an office supply store or copy center to have it laminated. Then you can be *together* at every meal.

38 Make a picture button pin—you know, the kind that people wear to athletic events, conventions, etc. Most award shops and elementary schools have the equipment available. Get a picture of the soldier in uniform and put a note under the picture that says, "I'm proud of my dad (or mom)." Make the button for the child to wear to school. Most schools would love to be a part of this by helping your child make the button.

39 Everyone loves getting presents, so another great way to stay in touch is by sending *care packages*. Big or small, they're always appreciated. They can arrive anytime and have anything edible in them. Make sure that what you send is wrapped very well to minimize the breakage. Also, realize that shipping times are long so don't send anything that will spoil. Some of the favorite items among soldiers are:
- Any appropriate food
- Beef jerky

- Small packaged snacks
- Candy
- Special traditional homemade goodies
- Grandmas® or Pepperidge Farm® cookies
- Single servings of flavored coffee, tea, or hot chocolate
- The hometown newspaper
- Small pouches of baby wipes (great for low water cleanups, and they smell like home)
- Pet flea collars (for the ankles) to help battle sand fleas
- Copies of children's school work so the parent can see what they are studying
- Pre-addressed, stamped postcards
- Phone cards
- Your family newsletter

40 "I send 'mini' scrapbooks from family events in a themed care package and usually include personal messages from family members."

41 "I send candy with fun, pun notes attached like: Gum—*I miss chew*; Mints—*We were mint to be together*; Lifesavers™—*You'll always be my lifesaver*; etc. Be creative."

42 When making cookies for care packages, remember to decorate them especially for the parent—it's something the children can do themselves. When you ship the cookies, remember to wrap them well.

Lisa shared a story with me about a family where the kids really wanted to remember their dad's birthday by making him a birthday cake like they did every year. But what good would the cake do at home? Not much— so they mailed it! An iced birthday cake, complete with candles, was boxed and shipped thousands of miles away through the postal system. It certainly paints an interesting picture.

Speaking of pictures, Mom was on top of things enough to take a Polaroid® picture of what the cake looked like *before* it was sent and included it in the box. Why do you think this mom went along with the idea of mailing a cake? "Because," she said, "sometimes you just gotta give in." Good for her!

43 This next idea falls under the "Have a Plan" heading and has to do with schoolwork. Challenges arise when all of a sudden the parent who used to help with this is no longer available. Lisa says the key to keeping schoolwork current is to set up a plan ahead of time. When the spouse who is left at home is not able to help in certain areas (for me it would be math), then find someone who can. Look to grandparents, neighbors, tutors, or their classroom teacher to fill in. Maybe you can even answer some questions during whatever brief phone time you have with them. Lisa says that putting a plan in place ahead of time helps with the fights that arise over homework and even chores around the house.

The following idea fits here, although it's not a part of my conversation with Lisa. It comes under pre-planning. I've discovered that legal and medical issues can become a different kind of problem for families with stepparents. If the parent is deployed and a stepparent is left behind, there could be legal problems for authorizing medical care. An organization of volunteer lawyers developed a *Family Member Pre-deployment Checklist* to help with these and other situations. The website link can be found in the back of this book under *Resources and Support.*

44 Consistency in daily lives plays a big role in keeping the peace at home. Sometimes Lisa gets some touchy questions and maybe you've had this happen, too. She talked about an eight-year-old boy who, during his free time, always liked to play Army. When his dad was deployed, his mom thought that maybe it would be better to have him stop playing this game because it was now "too close to home."

However, it was suggested that he should not stop playing because it was a constant in his daily routine— and now it could be a way to stay connected to Dad. Lisa took it a step further and suggested that Dad could be involved by creating some fake "tactical plans" before he leaves—perhaps basing them on football strategies. Then his son could play out these plans with his own army. It's a true connection in the *real* world.

Lisa, thank you for being a part of this project and for giving families in all branches of the military such insightful strategies for staying together—even when separated.

*"If you take care of the people,
the people will take care of the mission."*

—Sondra Albano, Ph.D.

Chapter 2

Ideas for the Deployment Phase

Service families are likely to experience separations stemming from short-notice deployments, frequent active duty assignments and relocations, long hours, shift work, and the uncertainty of where they will be next month. While this is an accepted part of a military career, it's not as commonplace for those who are called to duty from civilian forces. Deployment becomes a time of readjustment.

During deployment, many people would say that the most difficult thing to deal with is being separated from their families. It's probably the hardest thing the families have to contend with, too. During this time the miles can seem endless. Learning some of the techniques available for staying connected will help to shorten those miles.

Thinking of You

45 In an interview with Tara, she said that when her husband was overseas she knew he could call once a week for only 15 minutes. What was even more frustrating was that, for security purposes, the call was on an "automatic hang up" timer and would cut off the call at exactly 15 minutes—no matter where they were in the conversation! It was hard to try to think of all she wanted to tell him, such as what bills were paid, what the baby did since the last call, etc.

Here's a good suggestion for dealing with this situation: Buy a tiny spiral notebook and write things down as they occur. Carry the notebook with you. Then when you get the call, you can be efficient with your time because you'll already know what you want to talk about.

46 This is a quick, simple and inexpensive connection idea. You can do it for $1.75 and about 30 seconds of your time. Buy a decal that reflects the branch of service that you're in. It can be either an insignia decal or the spelled out name like a college decal. Then place it in the back window of your car. When you are driving and look in your rearview mirror, it will be a quick, happy reminder of your service member. Believe me, it makes you smile.

47 Shared tastes in music among family members is an emotional way to stay in touch. In most circumstances, servicepersons have CD players or audiotape players. Most likely, you have one or both at home, too. Burn a couple of CDs or record tapes of special songs from over the years for each of you to play while away. When my son went to college, I made a CD of piano music because Bryan used to fall asleep to that music in the car when he was little. It calms him when he plays it as background music. Sometimes you can just burn a few songs and send what you think each other will like.

48 A good tip for a deployed parent is to make up a *Memory Box* filled with special things of yours (as well as things that mean something to your children) so that they can go through it occasionally to feel like you're there. Many of those items will have your "scent" on them, and that's an extremely powerful tool to bring you right into the room.

If you have the time before you leave, consider going one step further while creating your *Memory Box*. Spend about an hour with your family and decorate the outside of the box in something fun and colorful. This will make it even more personal. Then, together, collect the special things that will go into the box.

49 Select a pre-set time each day for family members to think about each other for just a moment. This will be your own private "together" time. There is a scene in the animated movie *An American Tail* where the mice characters are separated from each other. At night they look in the sky and know that no matter what, they are together because they are looking at the very same moon.

50 With soldiers and families in different time zones, set one of the clocks in your home to the time zone of where the serviceman is. This makes it easier to look at the clock and think of what they might be doing at that moment.

51 **P.S. I Love You!** It might not be something they admit, but many men report that they enjoy getting affectionate little surprise notes. At the end of those notes add a "P.S." It increases the charm. There's something nostalgic about the P.S. that people respond to. It's that special afterthought like when you were at camp and your mom wrote, *P.S. I love you;* or the note your high school sweetheart slipped into the back of your notebook.

Because I Understand

52 There is one common thread that seems to hold military marriages together through times of separation. One of the best things to do while spouses are overseas is to become part of a support group made up of those who remain at home. Look for people on base or in your Guard unit. This is a great opportunity to meet with others who truly know what you're going through. Sometimes you feel like the outside world can't possibly understand the magnitude of what you're feeling. You need this group to share the everyday challenges you're experiencing, or when you're feeling out of control. Occasionally you just need a break, and a support group can help by

- getting together for coffee;
- listening while you just let loose and yell;
- babysitting so you can get away on your own;
- sharing what they know about services available;
- exchanging good fiction books;
- sending encouragement via email by forwarding inspirational messages to each other; or
- hosting social events to cement your connection as a continuous support network.

Remember that support systems are only effective if they are used. Most military spouses who remain behind are gifted with a tremendous amount of spirit and courage. They feel a sense of acceptance that "this is what we do." But even with that self-sufficiency, please take advantage of these support groups. They'll be enormously helpful during the times when you find that your "acceptance attitude" is waning; and when you're feeling positive, that spirit will be a lifting force for others.

53 Buy your child's favorite cookies or small pieces of candy like a Hershey's Kiss® or peanut M&M's®. When they miss you, tell them they are allowed to eat **just one** candy or cookie. (Limits are advisable.)

54 Many children I spoke with have a "Hug Friend" around. This is a special stuffed animal just for the purpose of hugging whenever the parent isn't there and they feel the need to hug something. Since our sense of smell is an effective connector, you might "spritz" the stuffed animal with some of your perfume or after shave.

55 Family Support Centers usually offer suggestions for stress management. When you're the one left behind, you have to realize how imperative it is for you to learn how to do little things for yourself that help to lessen your own stress. Is there a Health and Wellness Center (HAWC) near you, maybe on base? These centers provide information and services that will keep you fit and mentally/emotionally together during the separation.

One woman related that she thinks these centers are the military's best kept secret, and for now she's glad because then there's never a wait at the massage chair! She packs her three little ones in the car and heads over there about once a week. The babysitting service watches the kids while she gets a 45-minute stress relieving massage in a warm and relaxing atmosphere. This is HER time and she deserves it. She says that more spouses should give this a try.

For Better or Worse – Spouses...Are You Listening?

Many of the ideas in this book involve how to stay connected to the children. That's important because it's difficult for younger children to actually understand the logic behind the deployment. They just know that their moms or dads are gone. With spouses, it's another matter. There's a special kind of love that's missing for a while. The void that's left is on a deeper level. Taking special care to stay connected reinforces that you're "babysitting their hopes and dreams" until they return.

In interviews with Tara, Julie-ann, and other wives, I learned that they're married to wonderful men who took the time to find unique ways to show how much they care when they're on assignment. I'm pleased to have permission to share these ideas, along with those from others. As a spouse who is either leaving or staying behind, you can personalize the following suggestions to the particular needs of your own relationship.

56 Julie-ann loves the little Reese's Peanut Butter Cups®. Sometimes it just takes one to satisfy her craving for a taste of chocolate. Dave knows this. When he's on an assignment that takes him away for one or two weeks, he buys one peanut butter cup for each day he's away. Before he leaves, he hides them around the house so he knows Julie-ann won't find them. Then, each night when he's able to quickly phone home, he tells her where **just one** peanut butter cup is hidden. He said that if he told her all the hiding places at once, she'd eat them all! What a great way to make each call special.

57 Write a *Legacy Letter*. This is where you start a few sentences of a letter when you get up in the morning and then add sentences throughout the day when you have something special to say. This legacy letter can be composed over a week's time to give you more time to work on it. At the end of the day—or week— you've written a legacy that makes your spouse feel like they've been with you all day long.

Here's what one woman, an HQ key wife said about *Legacy Letters*: "I have my wives do the legacy letters. That way they are writing a letter over time and they have something to send, even when they think they have nothing to say. My husband and I have been doing this over the past 12 years. We started in boot camp. We feel that this way we miss nothing...because we write things down we would otherwise forget."

58 Deb bought a small heart-shaped, fabric-covered box at a hobby store and filled it with tiny gummed heart stickers—one for each day her husband would be gone. She sent it with her husband along with the instructions that each morning he was to take out a heart, lick it, and stick it some place...any place...on his body! That let her wonder all day where that special heart was, and the guys stationed with him got a big kick out of it too.

59 A friend of mine did this for her college student, but it will work just as well in your situation. She got it out of a magazine and called it a *Heart Attack*. She cut lots of different sizes of hearts out of colored construction paper. Then she wrote a *love phrase* (such as "You Doll" or "Cutie" or "Love Me") on each heart just like the little candy valentine hearts. She put about 50 or so in a big envelope and mailed it. When her husband pulled out all these hearts, it was like big *love* confetti. Here are some words that you can use to get started on your own "heart attack."

Miss You	Cool!	True Love
My Way	I Hope	Be True
Real Love	All Mine	Be Mine
Dear One	Love You!	One Kiss
Magic	Cutie	U R Kind
My Man	Smile	My Love
Kiss Me	Dream	So Fine
I Do	How Nice	U R A Star

60 Dave set up a *treasure hunt* around the house before he shipped out. He bought his wife a special gift that he hid as the treasure. Then he designed a series of clues, each one leading to another, until she eventually found the gift. On one of his phone calls home, he helped her guess the location of the first clue. She found it before he hung up, then had fun completing the treasure hunt after the phone call—prolonging the connection.

61 Here's one for the spouse who remains at home. Record an audiotape reflecting on all your favorite romantic memories—*the time we danced* *in bare feet on the roof of our apartment building; the moment Jimmy was born and I touched your cheek; etc.* It's just between the two of you, so anything goes.

62 Start a *Grateful Journal.* It's simple. Set up a computer file, or use a nice blank journal from the bookstore. Each day write three different things that you appreciate about your spouse. At the end of the week, email or *snail mail* that list to them.

63 This idea is a variation of the *Grateful Journal.* "Once when David was on TDY for six weeks," shares Julie-ann, "he kept a daily journal of his happenings and thoughts about me. Then he gave it to me when the six weeks were over. It was a very special gift!"

64 "My husband wanted a year's worth of Hershey® Kisses – put in a bag and sent to him – so he would have a 'kiss' per day."

65 When one airman was on a shorter assignment that took him away for five nights, he prearranged to have five different people (one for each day) help him with his plan. Sometime during each day he was gone, he had a different person call or stop by their home to say that he loved her and missed her. At first it was a complete surprise, but his wife finally caught on to his scheme after a couple of days and looked forward to hearing from her husband through his next messenger.

66 Create a tasteful "pinup" calendar of yourself for your husband.

67 One wife bought a tiny pocket photo album on a key chain (about 1" X 2" sized for small wallet photos) and filled it with little photos from all the best times of their lives—including a "sexy" pose. She sent it to him because it would fit so neatly into his pocket.

68 Carolyn wears a special charm around her neck and she can touch it whenever she's missing him or just needs to be thinking of him.

69 Lori made a "deployment pillow" for her husband and made one for herself, too, so that she has it at home. These pillows have little pockets, and in the pockets they placed favorite photos and poems they had written.

70 "To show my independence, and so he wouldn't worry, I sent pictures of myself mowing the grass and doing new things I learned to do. But when he came home on R&R I acted helpless so he would know I still needed him. It was a lot of fun."

71 Keesha sent him his favorite of her outfits in a Ziplock® bag and told him to hold on to it and bring it home with him so she can wear it just for him.

72 "I sent my husband the Sports Illustrated Swimsuit Issue©, but I had pasted my picture over all the models' heads. My husband passed the magazine on to the other guys before he saw what I had done, and I heard from every guy how cool that was and how it broke the mood!"

73 One wife took a full-length photo, enlarged it, and cut it apart into a "puzzle" of body parts. She put a single puzzle piece in each card that she sent him so that in the end he would have a full picture of his wife in whatever outfit – or not – that he likes. Whatever works!

74 Betty wrote: "Before my husband left, he wrote 'I Love You and Miss You' on the bathroom mirror. I would see this every morning and it would help to make my whole day brighter. It stayed there for over two years while he was Homeland Defense."

75 Darlene took a flat white sheet and had her best friend trace her body on it, then sent the sheet to her husband in Iraq so he could feel like he was laying next to her. She also sent a cut-out felt heart to go with the drawing so that he knew that her heart belonged only to him.

76 This is a wonderful version of the *Legacy Letter*. "I had a cassette player in the car, so while I was going from one place to another on especially long drives, I would just talk to him and tell him about my day. I sent the tapes periodically to Iraq. I always started the message with the date and where I was going. Oddly, when he got them, the radio was playing in the background. He loved it and it came with the added benefit of this timely music.

77 Deanna told me, "My husband likes to cuddle in bed. So I had a picture taken of me lying in bed with his favorite nightie on. I put this onto iron-on transfers (you many need to use three or four depending on size) and ironed it onto one of those long body pillow cases. I sent it to him and he stuffed it with two pillows and now has a 'body' to cuddle with."

78 *Date Night* with Dad (or Mom) is great, but what about *Date Night* with your spouse? Whenever her husband was home, Julie-ann said they had a special night set aside for *Date Night* once a week. And even though it didn't always work out that often, that's what they tried for. Here's what she said about it: "Fight for it! Even if it's just out for an extended cup of coffee. Plan ahead or it will never happen. Have the babysitter all lined up even if you don't know where the two of you are going. It's important to budget for your *Date Nights*, too. If you don't set aside the money for at least the sitter, then it's too easy to find excuses."

There are advantages to a *Date Night*:

- It gives you an important time to reconnect and refuel for the next trip away from home.
- Making it a priority helps to relieve some of the guilt that exists with having to leave.

- An added benefit is that the whole family sees your commitment to each other, and that adds a secure feeling to the household.

To close this very special chapter, someone who has been through a number of deployments asked me to share some advice that she knows has made it a little bit easier. "A connection idea between spouses is to make sure that before deployment you do not put up a wall or start a dispute because it is emotionally easier to part when you're not mad at each other. Trust me, this is sometimes easier said than done. After deployment, no expectations should be put on each other, either. The transition back into the family is much easier when nothing is 'over' expected."

Let's Get Personal

It's difficult when you can't be there in person to experience the day-to-day changes that occur at home. Here are some ideas for audio and video recording, as well as journaling, to help your soldier be a part of all that happens:

79 Do you have a new baby? Have the spouse at home make an audio (or digital) recording of your baby's laughter while he or she is doing something fun. It's such a warm and wonderful sound. Along with the recording, include a written description of what activity the baby is doing that's sparking all of that delightful laughter.

80 The hardest thing about being away is missing milestones in a child's life. If your spouse is gone for your child's first haircut, tie a ribbon around a lock of hair and send it with a picture of the child getting the haircut. Here's something else a young mother did for her husband during his year-long assignment. Their daughter was born a month after he left so she did hand drawings (as in idea #1) of her daughter's hands as a newborn and mailed the drawing to him. Then she did drawings again, progressively, for each month that followed. As he received each new pair of "hands" he could actually visualize how much she had grown over the year.

81 If there's a baby or toddler at home, be sure to have a video camera handy so your child's milestones can be recorded. Also, record what's happened in your child's growth while you were separated. That will make a great home movie for *Movie Night* when your soldier returns!

82 This idea is from Rebecca, who travels about half of her time for business. Although she may not be gone for extended periods of time the way a soldier would, she's away more often than many moms. "We started a journal for the kids to write in every day to let us know what they are doing. They write their thoughts on something they're happy or sad about, something that happened at school or home, etc. When I get home, it's a way to catch up on what happened while I was gone." They also might keep a journal of their accomplishments, awards, grades, etc. Have them write down some things that they want to do with the parent when he or she gets home. Writing things down tends to insure that they're not forgotten.

83 Try *Two-part Journaling*. It's very helpful to keep a journal of what you do together as it refers to a child's progress growing up. Because you're not together on a day-to-day basis, this serves as a reminder of the small steps that happen between the members of the family. It acts as cement for the times when you're not living together. The first part of the journaling is done while the soldier/parent is deployed. The second part is done when he/she returns by continuing to write in it together whenever possible.

It's All About Communication

Technology makes sending emails one of the best ways to stay connected. These pages talk about emails and telephones. It's a quick way to connect, and from my interviews, the most effective. Some phone calls are short, some are timed, and some are longer. But no matter what the length, nothing beats hearing the voice of the person you love.

Email is an incredible *real time* method of staying connected in a way that we haven't had available in past times of conflict. You can instantly send home words, images, and the security that your hands were on the keyboard only moments earlier, which means that you're alive and well. Email is a marvelous source for providing instantaneous connections from the field to relatives back home. It's a wonderful morale booster, so consider it one of your best forms of contact.

84 My challenge to you is to see if you can make those emails different. Break out of the mold within the realms of security restrictions. Send something funny, maybe a little outrageous, or something that the recipient would never expect. You might consider setting up a special phrase or saying that's just for your family, and include it in every email. You don't need to do something outrageous every time, just when you want a special pick-me-up.

85 Get instant messaging software on your computers. Then you can set times to chat in *real time* over the computer. I love being online in the middle of the day, hearing the chimes, and finding a message from my son. It's as good as a phone call, but you have to know when and where it's appropriate.

86 For emails, create an age-appropriate, fun quiz or questionnaire for your child to do when he/she signs on. Here are some suggestions for what might be included:
- Current events
- Friends
- Interests
- Activities
- Other favorite things

Make the quiz easy so they can't fail. People love to do quizzes. That's why short online quizzes and surveys are so popular. Remember back in school when you used to pass notes that had quiz questions that your best friend answered about your current crush?

87 For emails, have each of you answer the question: "What would you do with a million dollars?" Email your answers to each other. You might add something like, "You must have at least one truly goofy idea."

88 Children can formulate questions for their deployed parent to help de-mystify the destination and the daily experience. For example,

"How many sandbags a day can you fill?" or "How hot does it get at night where you are?"

Tip: A great resource for questions is *The Kid's Book of Questions* by Gregory Stock. Parents may want to get to know their kids better (and vice versa) by asking some of these questions before or during the deployment, either by phone or email. Some examples of questions:

- When someone says you are just like your mom or dad, do you like it?

- Do you try to be more like your parents or different from them?

- What was the most exciting thing you ever did on a dare? Are you glad you did it?

89 Along with emails, remember that you can also email greeting cards. There are lots to choose from and they often include fun animation and sounds. One of my favorite sites for online cards is www.bluemountainarts.com. There's a tab for email cards on the home page. Try one—it's addictive.

90 Every time you type a letter on the computer, whether it's to be printed and mailed or emailed, put a 2" X 2" family photo in the upper corner. Now every letter is even more special because each one comes with a memorable photo that can be saved and looked at often.

91 What else can you do on the phone? Talk to the kids before you leave and make a favorite song *your* song. When you call home, get the kids on the phone and sing your song together. One family chose *You Are My Sunshine.* It's simple, short, and filled with joy. That may stick in their minds (and yours) even more than words. You just may be an inspiration to those standing in line behind you waiting to use the phone!

92 Tim has been through four six-month deployments, so email has made all the difference in this recent deployment. Many nights he and his wife would email each other to discuss where they were going to meet in their dreams. He said, "Cheesy? Maybe. Effective? Absolutely!" Now that's the way to use email!

93 From computer programmer Carl Carlson, "If the cell phones your family use have text messaging, you can just leave a quick text message that says *I Love You,* and it doesn't require a response." Again, you can only do this where appropriate.

Finally, I offer some words of advice for using those precious 20 minutes of phone time. Each of you is having a difficult time with the separation. The spouse at home is dealing with the kids, illnesses, news, household questions, and loneliness. The deployed spouse is dealing with care and concern, fear of the unknown, and loneliness. Please be aware that it's hard to solve huge problems in this short time frame and could possibly leave you both uneasy. Hearing an uplifting voice on the other end of the phone, however, can do wonders for helping a soldier get through the rest of the day. These are 20 important minutes, so know ahead of time what you plan to talk about and be aware of the effect your words will have—both positive and negative. My advice is *Be aware and take care.*

Fun Projects to
Get the Kids Involved

You are the bows from which your
children as living arrows are sent forth.
The archer sees the mark
upon the path of the infinite,
and He bends you with his might that His
arrows may go swift and far.

Let your bending in the
Archer's hand be for gladness:
For even as He loves the arrow that flies,
so He loves also the bow that is stable.

—Kahlil Gibran from *The Prophet*

This is one of my favorite sections. I know that it's difficult to be away from your spouse when you leave because you miss the closeness that comes from being lovers. But you always know that your spouse, in a logical sense, understands the need for you to be away. With children, it's a different story. They may not understand. They just know that you're gone. What makes it even harder is the fact that young children don't have a very good sense of the reality of time. You can be gone for one week or one year and it's all the same to them.

55

The following is a wonderful way to help bridge the concept of time for the young ones:

94 Get a large empty jar (about the size of a quart of mayonnaise) and wash and dry it thoroughly. Here's what you put in the jar: For every day that the sailor will be gone, place one colored gumball in the jar. If he/she will be deployed for six months, then you'll place 183 gumballs in the jar. Then, beginning the day after he/she leaves, have the child take one gumball from the jar every day. As the level of gumballs goes down, the closer it is to the time your loved one will be home. Here are some variations to what you might put in the jar:

- Pieces of wrapped hard candies
- Peanut M&M's®
- Hershey's Kisses®
- Colorful marbles (only for children over five)

For children under age three, make a paper chain where one link represents each day of the assignment. To count down the time, tear off a link each day. One family wrote a "love note" on each link they took off, saved them, and gave them to their dad when he returned home.

Now let's look at a few things you might not have thought of—and even how the phone can make your child feel special. These are projects that kids can do so they will feel that their deployed parent will truly have a piece of them while away.

95 Another idea from Lisa White: Keep sending photographs, emails, and letters home. "Kids like pictures taken of the words *I love you*." How can you do that? Write it in shaving cream on a mirror, or draw it on paper or in the sand, and then take a picture of it. Maybe you can even spell it out in chocolate, pebbles, or pennies. Kids can be involved by using sidewalk chalk to write it on the driveway. Take a picture and send it to Dad or Mom.

96 Take young children out on a *treasure hunt* around the yard. Tell them to look for things that their soldier mom or dad might enjoy. This probably will include simple things like colorful leaves, small stones, blades of grass, etc. Put these together and send them. Don't discredit anything that a child finds, with the possible exception of something alive— like a caterpillar!

97 I remember when Bryan was in grade school, he would always come home with a joke he had heard that day. Remember those? They were the simple little jokes that kids thought were the funniest thing they had heard all day. Have your child write them down and email a silly "joke of the day" to your service member.

98 Have a favorite family sticker (like a fun sun, cartoon character, flower, bird, etc.) and make sure everyone has some. Then put one on every letter you send to each other. You might even stick one on the outside of the envelope. You can find some really cool ones at stores that sell scrap booking materials or from a company called Creative Memories®. (To locate a Creative Memories® consultant, you may visit www.creativememories.com.) And don't forget to seal your letter with a big kiss! Use lipstick or tinted gloss to make it even better.

More Fun Stuff and Projects

One of the best ways for children to keep the connection with deployed parents (and to know that their parents are thinking of them, as well) is to make them something that they can take with them. This section will provide more projects for kids, fun ways to use *snail mail,* and tips for helping your child get involved.

99 In our busy lives, it can sometimes be seen as a burden on our time to gather all the necessary materials for our children when they come to us saying, "I want to make something." It's easier to say, "Not now," than to hunt for the paper, paints, scissors, crayons, etc. So be ready ahead of time for all of the projects that your child may want to do on the spur of the moment. Assemble a *Craft Box* with everything they will need to be creative. Then when they get the call to create, they can get out the box, spread out a plastic tablecloth, and be ready to dig in. A large shoebox will serve as a *treasure chest* for everything they need. Here are some things you might want to include:

- Construction paper
- White copier paper
- School glue
- Scissors
- Pieces of felt
- Scraps of fabric and lace
- Buttons
- Sequins
- Glitter

- Pipe cleaners
- Macaroni shapes
- Paintbrushes
- Watercolor paint set
- Tissue paper
- Ribbons
- Wiggle eyes
- Rhinestones
- Small yarn pompoms
- Pieces of yarn
- Paper doilies
- Variety of stickers (hearts, stars, etc.)

You'll be amazed at the wonderful cards and projects that will come out of all this creativity. Projects are a wonderful way to make time go by, especially when you're missing someone.

TIP: Visit the hobby shop around each holiday to see what special holiday related stickers or craft items you can buy. It's much easier to find gummy heart stickers around Valentines Day, and snowflakes and Santas around Christmas.

100 Help your kids create their own stationery to use for special notes. Make it a simple self-mailer with lines for writing and a clip art picture from a computer publisher program. Print it on card stock paper, and you're all set to write. Personal stationery also makes a great gift to give to your child.

Email might be the fastest way to get a message home, but it isn't necessarily the most fun. For that, you have to be creative with *snail mail*. Years ago, that's all we baby boomers had available to us when we got mail.

Why do you think we often see photos or movies where a woman has a bundle of old letters tied with a ribbon in a safe place in her attic? We remember her picking them up ever so carefully and lifting them to her face to catch a whiff of long ago aftershave...all of this with a shimmer of a smile on her face. Technology has offered us the ability to communicate at the click of a button, which is wonderful, but please don't ever forget how amazing it is to receive a handwritten letter from someone you love.

Every time I'm speaking to a group of spouses and I talk about how heartwarming letters are, I see heads nodding throughout the room. What makes those letters so special? To begin with, it's the personal handwriting. No one else has your handwriting, so seeing it is a visual reminder of what you two share. The person who receives the letter can read it, then carefully put it in a pocket and retrieve it again and again to be reread when loneliness hits. Lastly, each letter often carries your scent on it. That scent alone can be just the lift they're looking for. Letters are romantic, personal, and a really fun memory to keep tied in a bundle!

When I was about 10 to 12 years old, I spent two weeks every summer at camp. My dad wrote me letters that I would get almost every day. That was how we stayed connected. What I liked best about his letters was that they were far from the ordinary. He did some interesting things with a pencil and paper. In fact, his letters were so much fun that other kids in my tent wanted to read them, too! When you're away long enough to send *snail mail*, try at least one of these approaches. Your kids will love it, and it will keep them busy for quite a while.

101 **Puzzle letters:** The simplest way to write this type of letter is to get out a sheet of plain copy paper, sit down, and write your letter. When you're finished, take a pair of scissors and cut it into about 15 odd shapes. If you don't have scissors readily available, you can tear it into pieces. Then put these pieces into an envelope and mail it home. Your child will have to put the *puzzle* together in order to read your letter.

Here's another alternative that the children can use for sending letters to you. I found a company called *Compoz-A-Puzzle* that manufactures a lightweight white cardboard pre-assembled jigsaw puzzle with about 9 to 24 pieces. Write a letter on this blank puzzle and then break the pieces apart and mail them. This paper comes in different sizes and with different sized pieces. You may contact them at:

> • Compoz-A-Puzzle, Inc.
> Glen Head, NY 11545
> 1-800-343-5887
> www.compozapuzzle.com

Here are two products carried by this company that can be used in variations of the above:

Puzzle Clonzz: Pre-assembled jigsaw puzzles that can be used with your computer's laser or inkjet printer.

Adrawables: These are great for kids who want to make something fun to send to you. They are "color-in" jigsaw puzzle greeting cards. The card fronts get colored in and signed, then broken apart and mailed. They come in different card collections like greetings, dinosaurs, spacecraft, sweethearts, and Christmas. These are perfect for children who like coloring books.

TIP: From the Family Readiness Center: When you write letters to a service member, number the letters *and* the envelopes in the order they were written. Sometimes the mail causes lots of letters to arrive at once, and the numbering system will alert the recipient to the order in which they were written. They'll make more sense!

102 Using Puzzle Clonzz, make a *real* jigsaw puzzle. Print a photo on a puzzle page, break it apart, and put it in a small box or envelope. Send it to your soldier or include it in a care package.

103 If you have a child over the age of about seven or eight, write and send a note to him/her in an easy, cryptic code (sort of like a cryptogram) with each letter being represented by the respective number of that letter in the alphabet.

A	B	C	D	E	F	G	H	I	J	K	L	M
1	2	3	4	5	6	7	8	9	10	11	12	13

N	O	P	Q	R	S	T	U	V	W	X	Y	Z
14	15	16	17	18	19	20	21	22	23	24	25	26

Here's an example:

8 9   11 1 18 12 1,
    9   13 9 19 19   25 15 21   1 14 4
12 15 22 5   25 15 21!
    12 15 22 5,   13 15 13 13 25

It says:

Hi Karla,

I miss you and love you!

Love, Mommy

104 Another thing my dad did for me was to take a piece of copy paper and fold the edges and sides around to form an odd shape. Then he'd write his letter to me on this folded paper. When done, he opened the paper and sent it opened up or folded just once or twice. In order for me to read it, I'd have to figure out how to refold the letter the same way that he did. It made receiving mail a real adventure.

105 "We made a 'Daddy Mailbox' for my son's room. Every time he wants to send mail to him he puts it in the mailbox and puts the flag up. It is always gone in the morning. Then my husband will send him stuff and I put it in the mailbox for him."

106 Give each child a different color or type of envelope that only they can use to send a letter to their parent. (Get them at the Dollar Store). It's fun and it makes it easier for the parent to locate a specific letter they want to re-read.

Special Ideas for Younger Children
(under 10)

107 "I had my children lie down on a large sheet of paper like the kind you get on newspaper end rolls. Then I traced around their bodies and cut them out. Each child colored and decorated theirs and wrote special messages to their dad. They were then folded up and mailed to him."

108 How fun and easy for the little ones. Have them use finger paint and make thumbprints on a piece of paper. They can take crayons and make little bugs out of them if they want. Have Mom write the words "Thumbody loves you!" at the bottom of the page and send it off.

109 "Daddy Notes" or "I Love You" notes. "My husband writes them to the kids before he leaves and gives them to me. I give the notes to the kids daily at breakfast. He also does this while he's home but at work every day. The kids love them!"

This idea brought tears to my eyes—as do most of them!

110 Have him leave an unwashed t-shirt (only worn once) and slip it over the child's pillow as his/her pillowcase.

Quite a few of the ideas I received involved the use of a stuffed bear. They were all great ideas so I placed them in their appropriate sections of the book. This is probably an idea that would work for children of any age.

111 "Before my husband left, he gave each of our daughters a stuffed bear and told them to every day *'Hug your bear and say your prayers!'* Whenever he called or wrote to them, he told them that he could feel their hugs."

112 This idea is one you can pull out during deployment when things are reaching a low and the family needs a pick-me-up. Have a "pajama day." The family does things together and no one gets dressed! You have a great big pajama party – popcorn, movies, games, fun foods, etc. It's amazing how much it helps just to be silly and laugh.

Special Ideas for
Older Children and Teens
(over 10)

This falls under the category of "Just something you should be aware of." I've heard from a number of mothers of teens who felt they had good relationships with their kids. However, something changed about a month prior to their parent's deployment.

The best way to describe it was that the child began to pick fights and start arguments over the smallest things. A home that might normally be running smoothly now was suffering lots of waves. Most of these arguments were between them and the deploying parent. It seemed as though he/she could do nothing right! Moodiness prevailed and it became truly frustrating. The parent wanted things to go well because he/she knew they wouldn't be seeing each other for a long time and didn't want to leave on uneasy terms.

Finally, one mom went to her 17-year-old son and laid it on the line. She demanded to know what accounted for his abrupt change in behavior at a time when things needed to be as upbeat as possible.

Her son blurted out, "I figured that it would be easier for both of us if we were mad at each other when he has to go!"

Oh...she had never even thought about the logic and emotion of that statement. Now it became clear that the feelings were out and they could talk together about the deployment from here and that anger was not the way to get by.

If you have teens and pre-teens whose behavior toward the deploying parent is changing, you might consider that they are using the same logic. Often the older ones tend to internalize how they're feeling about the absences. It's difficult for the parent at home to try to reach them to help. Lots of times they worry about something that they truly don't need to and that doesn't help anything. It just adds to their stress. Here's an idea that a youth counselor at a Family Readiness Group shared with me that allows a parent to step in and help them deal with the emotions they're feeling:

113 Have the child make a list (as specific as possible) of all the things they are worried about regarding the deployment. It's a good idea to have the at-home parent sitting with them, but they shouldn't contribute to or edit any of what's being listed. Next, have the child take list #1 and divide it into two separate lists: the first is a list of things they **can** do something about, along with ideas of steps they can take. This is where a parent can help, but only to act as a sounding board or to help generate the action steps. The second list contains the things you have no control over and can do nothing about. Then encourage the child to allow themselves to let go of what's on this second list and only focus on those things they **can** control. That should take some of the burden off.

I absolutely love this next one! If you have teenage girls at home this is a must. I'm so impressed that the recruiting office was willing to take part in this.

114 "On Valentine's Day, one of the ladies in my unit had a recruiter in the area go in uniform to her teenage daughter's school and deliver roses from her dad. She felt so special and loved."

115 "My teenagers like to go out to eat, so on Sunday mornings we'll all go to IHOP® to eat pancakes. Over breakfast and coffee we read the Sunday paper and discuss the week's events while sharing our feelings and opinions. It allows for quality time and lets us catch up after a busy week and start a new one feeling connected."

116 Let the teenager put together a video or DVD of important events that are happening during deployment and have them do a narration.

117 Have your teenagers use their computer skills to create a family newsletter, either online or on paper. Make it one page and fill it with events from the family. Include an interview with a grandparent, movie reviews, question of the week, list of birthdays, jokes, or just thoughts of the day. Put an issue out every couple of weeks or every month.

118 Write a short letter to your child relaying some of your thoughts about the time they were born and the events of the day leading up to it, such as who was doing what, etc. Bryan has always loved to hear about how his dad was playing baseball when I had to go to the hospital, how he was born one minute before midnight, and how he was *almost* an Easter baby. This story never grows old.

119 Write down a short list of "Best advice I got from...(Mom or Dad)" and email or *snail mail* the list to the parent. This kind of thing makes deployed parents feel super good. It lets them know that even from a distance, they are able to have influence on what their children learn.

Many of the emails that came to me talked about having the older ones create some kind of mentor program in the unit or FRG. This lets them mentor and help with the feelings of the younger children. It would work something like the *Big Brothers Big Sisters* program. They can also organize a peer group that would meet once a month during unit meetings in a room by themselves. It's interesting how helping others can lessen the pain you're going through yourself.

I'm taking a break here to share a poem with you. If you read the first edition of *I'm Already Home*, you saw it there, too. I decided to keep it in this version because it sends a strong and important message to all parents. It made me think about how much we tend to get wrapped up in our own day-to-day lives and don't pay as much attention as we should to the activities of our kids. As parents we need to take a longer look at our kids. Let them know that we will always be there for them, to guide them and offer a smile of support whenever it's needed.

Innocence was written by Molly Waneka, who was a high school senior at the time. She wrote it in the week following the student shootings at Columbine High School in Colorado. Every parent should read it.

Innocence

Did you notice what I was wearing to school today?
Did you even bother to look my way?
Did you realize it might be your last chance
to give your child one...last...glance?

As soon as I step out that door
I am exposed to the world's deadly roar.
You have taught me not to be frightened,
but what about the other kids' parents,
who aren't quite as enlightened?

Do I have the chance of being in danger
and in the path of someone's release of anger?
Is there anything else you expect of me?
Because I expect the world to have more sanity.

At the end of the day, will we all return home?
Or because of the insanity, will someone be left alone?
When I go outside, is it okay to laugh?
Or will I be breaking the silence of
some tragedy's aftermath?

Can a child still have dreams and goals
without first being frightened for the
safety of their souls?
Can I have your word that I can live another day?
Or is that a subject in which you have no say?

Did you notice what I was wearing to school today?
Did you even bother to look my way?
Did you realize it might be your last chance
to give your child one...last...glance?

71

Thanks, Molly, for reminding us always that life is fragile and that we all have to remember to take the time to pay attention to each other—parents and children alike. Remember that our children **do** want us to spend time with them. We can't kid ourselves into thinking otherwise—nor should we.

Pets and Deployment

We just finished talking specifically about projects for kids. This seems like the perfect time to talk about pets...because kids just go with pets. I recently had the pleasure of speaking at Family Readiness conferences in Kansas, Ohio and Michigan. At the breakout session in Kansas, a woman asked me if I had ever talked about the affect that deployments have on pets. I admitted that I hadn't ever given it much thought, primarily because I didn't have pets. Well, that started a great discussion. After that I decided I had to find out more and share it. During those discussion sessions I learned what pet owners are doing to help their animal family members feel integrated during the separations. Their ideas are shared below.

120 The sense of smell is the main way most animals stay connected. "My husband is currently deployed and I took one of the T-shirts he had worn (so it still carried his scent) and put it in the dog's bed so he can curl up in it. Or you can make a new bed out of a sack of old t-shirts."

121 Ask local retirees to help with horses and the tasks of larger animals—like riding and brushing them. This keeps the horse in constant contact with someone.

122 "We gave our dog a new 'comfort toy' while my husband was gone. A comfort toy could be something that belonged to him like an old slipper or shirt knotted up like a chew toy."

123 "We actually made a video of our soldier calling our pet and talking to him. We can put it in the VCR and the dog sits and watches!"

124 "I discovered that the dog began to ignore commands from me after my husband left. Because he was the one who usually disciplined our dog, I asked my husband to send a cassette tape with his voice 'barking out' various commands like *Sit, Stay,* and *No.* Whenever the dog stops taking me seriously, he'll follow the commands on the tape."

125 Dana and her husband don't have children, so she dresses the dogs up for a special holiday picture and makes a card out of it for that holiday.

126 From Carrie: "My dog gets depressed about a month into Ken's deployments. When this happens, I give her a *Daddy T-shirt* and Ken will talk to her on the phone. It actually helps."

127 Have a Pet Rodeo with other "pet" families in your unit. Offer fun activities at a community location. It's play time for the pets, and a social time for family members left behind.

128 "Our armory video tapes messages to our soldiers. We're alloted five minutes and it's instantly sent via email to the soldiers. Quite a few families brought in the dogs and cats and had them be a part of the message."

After this event, I talked with an animal behaviorist, Dr. Suzanne Hetts, who was not the least bit surprised at hearing that the family pet was "moping" around the house. Her insights are a wonderful and helpful look into pet behavior and how to condition your pets ahead of time to the pending separation. Here's what she suggests:

"A serviceperson's deployment causes upheaval not only for human family members but for pets as well. Pets can be sensitive to any kind of change in routine, whether it be a move to a new residence, a new baby, a change in work schedule, addition of another family pet, or being boarded when the family goes on vacation.

"Just as people do, pets vary in their ability to adjust to changes. Some seem to be barely affected, while others may show significant changes in behavior. If your pet's behavior has changed, keep in mind it may not be in direct response to your serviceperson's absence. Your pet may also be reacting to the changes in your family's behavior and routine. By reading our body language, pets can tell if we are angry, sad or anxious. So your pet may think something is 'wrong' based on your behavior, and display anxious, threatening, or fearful behaviors of his own.

"It's much better to try to prevent a problem reaction to a military absence than it is to try to resolve any resulting behavior problems after they occur."

129 "Start by being proactive. Try to anticipate what changes in routine your pet might experience once your spouse leaves. For example, will your pet be left alone more often? If so, begin to prepare your pet for this now. Dogs are generally much more sensitive to being left by themselves than are cats. Begin to purposefully leave your dog alone for short time periods every day if possible— perhaps 15 minutes or less at a time. Daily practice with being left alone helps your dog learn how to tolerate being by herself, rather than this being a rare event that she doesn't have the skills to cope with. When you leave, give your dog a special food-filled toy, like those seen on our website (http:// www.animalbehaviorassociates.com/pet-owner-products.htm#toys). This will help your dog think that being left alone is a 'good thing', not an unpleasant one. Pick the toy up as soon as you return.

130 "Is your deployed serviceperson the only (or primary) one who feeds or plays with your pet or takes your dog for a walk? If this is the case, begin to have other members gradually assume more and more of these responsibilities *before* your soldier leaves. If your pet is more attached to the spouse who will be leaving than to other family members, try to shift this attachment onto others. Someone other than the serviceperson should become the source of pleasant experiences, whether that be play, petting or feeding.

131 "If your spouse is already deployed and your pet is having problems, first try to make the pet's routine as similar as possible to what it was prior to your spouse's absence. Getting back to as normal as possible often helps not only pets, but you as well. Take time to do things with your pet that she particularly enjoys, whether that's being brushed, taken for a walk, or played with. These activities may also help make you feel better.

132 "Avoid giving your pet more attention when she is hiding or inactive. That only teaches your pet that those behaviors 'work' to get your attention. Instead, encourage your pet to do things she likes to do, as mentioned previously.

"If your pet stops eating or shows any other sign of illness (such as loose stools or soiling in the house) a trip to the veterinarian is in order. Stress can sometimes cause physical illness, or your pet may have become ill coincidental to your spouse's departure, not because of it. If necessary, your veterinarian can even prescribe a course of short-term anti-anxiety medication to help your pet over the first few difficult weeks.

"Separation reactions in pets are often self-limiting. Within a few weeks or a month, you will likely find your pet is back to his old self. It's well known that pets are good for our physical and mental health. As you help your pet adjust to your serviceperson's absence, you may find that you take comfort in your pet's trusting presence and unconditional love."

Printed with permission of Dr. Suzanne Hetts

Ideas for Extended Family Members

As I think of caregivers, babysitters and others who are actively involved with the lives of the families, I thought it would be nice to share some ideas especially for them. I've heard lovely stories about how a grandparent, neighbor or co-worker has made a difference. Some of them just need to be shared with you. I never want us to forget that the word "family" extends far beyond the borders of the house.

133 Create a name bracelet with letter beads spelling out your loved one's name, making the rest of the bracelet out of standard beads, such as glass, plastic, or even sterling silver. You can put a personal charm on the clasp, if you'd like.

A women's group in Jackie's church made red, white and blue plastic bead bracelets on an elastic cord with James' (Jackie's deployed husband) name on it. They made enough for any person in the church who would like to wear one—and they wore them until James came home. Every day as they put them on, they said a prayer.

134 Another family went to www.bracelets america.com and created cuff bracelets similar in design to the original POW/MIA bracelets of the '60s. Each family member's bracelet had a

specific saying meaningful to the person wearing it. This truly helped them feel a personal connection to the absent serviceperson.

135 Suggestion from Christine: Set up an Ofoto® account. The deployed spouse and every member of the family can download pictures to this location. Each person has an individual password to access the site. Pictures can be ordered from them so that each family member can have the pictures they want. It's so convenient.

136 A real time saver: Pass along your ideas and needs for care packages—especially themed packages. Brainstorm with each other so that you are not all sending the same things. It just takes a bit more coordination.

137 Another idea that makes sense: Assign a day of the week to each member of the family, including the little ones. For example, Monday goes to the sisters, Tuesday to the brothers, Wednesday belongs to the parents, Thursday to a child, etc. On that day, once a week, the person assigned is responsible for sending something or staying connected in some manner with the soldier, airman, marine, or sailor. It can be just an email, but it's something! This plan helps distribute the challenge of staying connected and also gives the serviceperson something to look forward to each day of the week! Better yet, no one is left out of the loop.

138 Take a bed sheet and trace family members' hands all over it. Have them each write a message in a fabric pen to the loved one. Send it along with a big note that says to "wrap up" in everyone's protective hands.

139 Here's one from a truly involved mom whose son and daughter are serving as Captains: "This is a variation on *Flat Daddy*. I always kept a disposable camera with me and a sign that said 'Hi Megan.' I took pictures with just about everyone—work, family, neighbors, at parties, etc. Then I put them in an album and sent the album to her. It really connected all the folks supporting her and supporting us."

140 This is a very creative idea! A family made a photo collage on a blank clock face with a picture of a family member, including the serviceperson, at each "hour" position. That way they were with each other "for all time." You can get wall clocks with blank faces at hobby shops, or just buy a simple one at a discount store, remove the front, and trace one from the face that came with the clock.

141 A slight variation of a good idea passed along to me: "I sent my husband in Iraq a CD with lots of songs. Then we got together and as a family wrote a handwritten letter that incorporated the title of each and every song on the CD! It was really silly but it sure made him laugh...and that was the goal. When this is done with the creative input of the entire family, it's not only a blast to create, but the letter is even better with many minds working on it."

142 Let all family members get involved in putting together a family newsletter once a month. Send it to the person on assignment, and have copies to hand out to friends in the community who might also like to be kept up to date.

Remember that as a family you're all in this together.

How Communities, Co-workers, Churches, Schools and Neighbors Can Help

I mentioned before that as a family, you're in this together. I know that as a community we're in this with you! Thousands of Americans around the country are asking what they can do to show support for all our service members serving on their behalf. What can we do that goes beyond sporting a yellow ribbon magnet on the car? Much more than you think.

Let me tell you about George. He's a wizened older man who works a farm in a rural community. Every time an airplane of our servicemen and women is scheduled to arrive at the small community airstrip, George heads out from the farm in the 1970 Chevy pickup truck that has seen better days.

He arrives at the airstrip and parks in the same spot at the end of the runway. He creaks open the rusty door and climbs out, but not before grabbing a large 5-foot American flag from the seat beside him. He walks around the truck to the tailgate and opens it as far as the old chain restraints will let it go. He briefly takes his hand and sweeps aside the pieces of hay and leaves that the wind has blown there, and taking his flag, he climbs into the bed of the truck.

The flag is on an old, battered wooden pole and he places one end into a bracket attached to the inside wall of the bed. The beautiful symbol of freedom unfurls in the breeze as George turns to sit on a cushion next to the flag and hears the familiar noise of the plane engine getting louder. He squints and shields his eyes from the sun as he watches the plane get closer.

The plane touches down at the dirt end of the strip just a couple hundred feet behind where George's truck is sitting. As the plane taxis past the truck George can see the smiling faces in the windows as he waves his arms, enthusiastically welcoming the soldiers and airmen home at last!

George has become a tradition. For two years he has driven his beat up old truck to that same spot at the end of the runway and welcomed home every serviceperson who has served from their community. He's been there in daytime and night, rain, snow, wind, and blinding sun. He's never missed a flight. George is the first person they see as they land, and for them he seems to embody the very reasons why they went in the first place. Bless you, George.

Perhaps going to the airstrip isn't how you define "getting involved," but there's a lot that can be done to help. Think about it; be creative.

I realize that since you own this book, you are probably the spouse in a military family. You might be thinking, "This part isn't written for me." That's true. It's written for those **around** you who would like to help.

As a military spouse, you are probably on the receiving end of well-intended requests from people for how they might help you or others. This section gives you some ideas of what other families have found most useful, and enables you to give some suggestions that are in addition to what you have personally come up with. Also, we all know of community churches, schools and organizations that want to help but don't know how. This section is available for you to pass along to any of them to get them started. They will be grateful to you for pointing them in the right direction.

Personally, I'd like to see these ideas help to close the gap between the military families and the civilian world around them. Many people who rely solely on the media for their knowledge of what's going on overseas just can't feel the impact of true understanding. The further away you get from a base or post, the more difficult it can be to help the community feel the personal impact that separation causes. It's often this lack of comprehension that can thwart even the best of intentions. Both sides need to be aware of this. As a neighbor, don't complain about how your husband forgot to take out the trash; it's insensitive to someone whose husband has been away for months. As a family member, it's important to keep in mind that comments like these are made innocently, and are not meant to be hurtful. Take a deep breath and smile! People really do care.

In this section I seem to talk more about Air and Army National Guard families than of other branches that tend to have a few more support services available on base. The Guard members are civilian soldiers and airmen who come directly from your neighborhood, church or community. They are the families you'll be more aware of on an everyday basis. Let's take a look at what some of these families have shared.

143 Kim Clark gave me permission to tell you you what they did in their armory: "We traced the outline shape of an 8" yellow ribbon magnet onto a piece of paper. Then we photocopied the drawing onto yellow paper and cut them out. We had lots of children and friends who wanted to do something for our soldiers other than writing letters, etc. We gave each of them a paper ribbon to decorate and write messages on. We ended up with about 3,000 ribbons colored and/or with messages so they were all different. We filled the armory from top to bottom so that when our soldiers returned home they had a huge and wonderful visual aid as soon as they walked in the big back door. Afterwards, that day or at their convenience, they were allowed to take any that their children and friends had designed.

We kept hundreds available at all times for school and church classes. The wall was an ongoing project so that we would always have all deployed troops covered. It was great because it almost put itself up and the soldiers gradually took it down so it didn't take a lot of manpower! Everyone loved it."

144 Are your children members of a group like the Girl Scouts, Boy Scouts, or church youth fellowship? Are they on a high school cheerleading team, a pompom squad, or the football or basketball team? They can provide such services as Easter egg hunts for children and baby sitting for parents to go Christmas shopping or for Family Readiness unit meetings. How about babysitting so that a parent can just get out and go to a movie with friends? They can also offer a hand in mowing lawns, raking leaves, or making small repairs to the home of a deployed soldier. There's so much for the young people to do!

145 "A number of servicepersons had returned to our community all at once. We got together and arranged to provide a full catered dinner for them and their immediate families just so they could relax with each other and we could welcome them home. We used one of the local VFW halls. We had signs made welcoming them and put them up all over town."

146 Have a couple of community families sponsor or "adopt" a family with a deployed member. Take part in their celebrations and create videos together to send to the soldiers/airmen. The community that did this stressed that the key is to help the family keep up their family traditions as much as possible. A variation of this is something a close neighborhood can do. Have one family host a casual get together for neighbors and set up a video camera. Then all the neighbors can make messages of thoughts, hellos, prayers, and hope. Send this DVD to the soldier along with copies of their neighborhood newsletters and hometown newspapers.

147 Attend a school sporting event, concert or recital where the children of deployed neighbors or co-workers are performing.

148 Are you baking cookies? Invite the "little hands" of a child to help. This takes some burden of childcare off of the parent for a moment and it's fun for you, too!

149 Do you have your own young children in your home, or grandkids who come to visit? Next time you're together, invite the deployed service member's kids over to play, if they are similar ages.

150 The wife of a deployed airman posts her family newsletters at work so her co-workers can be up to date and save her having to answer the same questions a lot. These same co-workers would also put together small "care packages" every two months as a thank you for her to send.

151 Neighbors: "Before my husband left on deployment, our friends made homemade cards, stamped the envelopes, and gave them to him as a gift with the sole purpose of having him send those cards to me and the kids. He's sent them about every week since leaving and it's the highlight of their week!"

152 What a great community: One of the wives of a deployed airman was to give birth soon and Dad couldn't be there. So the community held an old fashioned bake sale and raised enough money to fly in one of the wife's relatives to be with her instead! What a nice thing to do.

153 One city put up a huge community Christmas tree with lights on it at City Hall. All families were invited to make an ornament honoring their serviceperson who is currently deployed, or who had been deployed during the previous year. Then on a special night, just for them, with refreshments and music, all the families partied together and decorated the tree with their ornaments.

154 Compile a list of area licensed tradesmen such as plumbers, electricians, and landscapers who are willing to provide their services to the deployed families free of charge. This list can be left at City Hall to be accessed by the families. Along these lines, a city or town has deferred the water, sewer and garbage fees during the deployment. It is suggested that you contact the city council with the names and number of soldiers/airman who would be involved. They said that numbers do make a difference.

155 While one community in Kentucky was putting together care packages to send to Iraq, they also included many items for the troops to give away to the Iraqi children. They desperately need the items and especially love getting them. Consider sending things like Teddy bears and dress up clothes for them, pencils, crayons, paper, satchels or book bags, scissors, shoes, soccer balls, dolls, and hair ornaments like bows and barrettes. The servicepersons enjoy playing "Santa Claus" all year round.

156 An office gave a birthday party for the son of a deployed co-worker in honor of what his dad is doing for his country. They took pictures at the party and sent them to Dad. He loved it.

157 As a fun event, a small company held a silent auction and yard sale. The proceeds went to buy phone cards for the servicepersons and their families. At the event, instead of a guestbook, they had some greeting cards that were signed and sent overseas along with the phone cards.

158 Get a local florist to discount their price, or a local corporate sponsor to cover the costs, and have the florist offer to deliver flowers for a special occasion one time during the deployment/ assignment. Before he/she leaves, have the serviceperson jot down the event for the flowers, to whom they should be delivered, and the address.

159 Here is an email I received from Leslie: "I saw you on KUSI morning news. I'm a daycare provider and the parents of two of my children are currently deployed. I send them an e-mail every day that their children are in my care, along with a digital photograph, and tell each of them about our day...what we ate, what we did, and anything funny or new that their children are doing. They are very appreciative of my contact with them while they are at sea. We've made stronger friendships above the daycare provider/ parent relationship as a result."

There was nothing more moving to me than when I drove by a large open area in our community and saw over 5,000 American flags (large 3' X 5' flags on 8-foot poles) erected in pristine rows. Each flag represented a civilian who died in the WTC on September 11, the firefighters and emergency personnel who perished there, and one for every American and Coalition serviceperson who has sacrificed their lives in the fight against terror. Each of these flags had a yellow ribbon tied around the pole along with the name and hometown of each. The huge display was called the Healing Fields. I've never experienced anything like it, and I was so proud of my community for being a part of this memorial.

160 Keep expressing your thanks to the family for the sacrifice they are making so you can live free!

Looking for a family to help?
A National Guard Family Assistance Center (FAC)
can give you more ideas on how to help.
Check www.guardfamily.org for FAC listings.

Schools Are on Your Side

We talk quite a bit about how the family unit can stay strong and intact while someone is away on deployment or assignment. At home we can monitor any emotional changes that may occur in our children and be of whatever help we can. But what happens when our children walk out that door to school? After all, they are spending about eight hours of their day there. We have to be sure not to undervalue the role that educators play in the welfare of kids of all ages.

Sometimes a school either won't know what to do, or won't be aware of the families who have a person away from the home at any given time. So the first responsibility lies in your hands. Be sure to advise your school right away of the assignment and any behavior changes to watch for during that time. Be sure the administration AND the teachers are involved.

It's important to understand that they may not immediately know how to be of the most assistance. Now you can help them. Give them some of the following ideas that have been submitted by parents from around the country. They say that these help the transition for the child and also the understanding and acceptance of the other students in the classroom. Teachers, being the special people they are, are always looking for ways to help.

161 As we talk about informing the school, let me show you a "template" of a letter that a Guard unit composed that is sent by the parent to the school to alert them of the impending deployment or long-term assignment. You might find it helpful. Remember, use it as a guideline only. You can personalize your own the way you need it to read. This is to get you started.

{Date}

Dear {Teacher or Principal},

The father/mother of _____ is being deployed with his/her National Guard Unit and will be gone for an undetermined amount of time. I make you aware of this because you may notice some behavioral, emotional, or academic changes. _____ may act out, be more/less active, or withdraw from friends and activities he/she once enjoyed. Emotionally he/she may be angry, sad, or anxious or may be hiding that anything is bothering him/her. Academically, he/she may find it difficult to concentrate which may cause grades to dip. Also, with one parent absent, there may not be anyone to help with homework. If you notice any of these things, please do what you can to support my son/daughter and keep me informed. Please alert the school counselor and nurse of this situation, as well, as their support may also be needed. Thank you in advance for the many ways your tender care and attention will help my son/daughter cope throughout this very stressful period.

Sincerely,

{Parent signature and phone number}

Helpful Resources:
{State} National Guard State Youth Coordinator
1-800-000-0000 {Attach business card}
www.guardfamily.org National Guard Family Programs website

162 The most common idea, which was submitted over 50 times, is to have a school or classroom "adopt" a soldier, airman, or even an entire unit. It's usually the parent(s) of children in the class, but he/she can certainly be someone not affiliated with a classmate. Some of the things the class can do are to write letters, do things for their family here, help them celebrate special occasions like Christmas and birthdays, make baked goods to send, become pen pals if there are several "adoptees," and send notes about the activities that the students are doing in the schools. Don't forget to send a class photo and small album showing the kids and their activities, and how about a DVD or CD of them singing songs, reciting essays, etc. Then they can truly feel involved.

163 If there is a student in your class with a deployed parent (or even several children), have that soldier/airman mail the classroom a flag that had been flown over their camp for a day.

164 Connect the school with recruiters or public affairs officers in your area. Ask them to come to the school to "train" the staff on how to be aware of emotional issues that are likely to arise and how they might help.

165 One school made a flag out of student handprints and wrote the names of service members inside the handprints. You could do this and send it to the unit or display it in the school.

166 Lynn shared this amazing idea with me, and since she's letting me share it with you, I'm relaying it in it's entirely just as she wrote it to me. "We come from a small community in North Dakota. When my husband was on a year long remote assignment to Kuwait, I had to do something special for Christmas. He was very involved at the school my kids attended. So here's what I did. First I used the die cut machine and cut out about 400 Christmas light shapes. Then I sent a package to school for every teacher and asked that every student and teacher either decorate or write a note on the light bulb. Once I had collected the bulbs, I strung them on a piece of string and mailed them to my husband. The children did anything from drawing pictures of Ninja® Turtles to saying "Be Safe." When her husband received his lights, he shared them by having them hung in the chow hall. Guys couldn't read more than five or six without a tear coming to their eye. This could be done in a parish community for any holiday. The words of encouragement mean the world."

167 Here's one from Rob in California: "Yea for the Girl Scouts! They come through every time, and this was just a special way. In a community school where there were many active duty Guard troops, the Girl Scouts set to selling cookies. They printed up their own order forms and at the bottom of the form they put: ☐ *Check here if you want a box to go to Iraq.* Suddenly they had 3,000 boxes allocated to be sent. Be careful of what you ask for because soon the 3,000 boxes became 22,000 boxes of cookies!

"The Girl Scouts put 'Operation Cookie Drop' into action and began packing cases of cookies. They went a step further. In each case they included a disposable camera along with a pre-paid envelope to send the cameras back so they could 'meet' the servicepersons who were enjoying the cookies. Now how on earth do you ship all those cases of cookies? You go out to the community. A local radio station raised the money to ship them all over the world! Now the Girl Scout troop has a picture of the Delta Force Special Forces smiling with their cookies!"

168 Here's another project for the class. Take a bed sheet and have the kids from a class or the whole grade paint or write support messages on it, and then send it overseas. It can be done for a single person, or sent to a unit. The unit responds back in various ways—usually with pictures, notes, or special little trinkets. This builds great support and connection.

169 School clubs hold community service projects as fundraisers, such as hosting a dance at the middle school for money for phone cards. One DECA club chose "penny wars" to support a local FRG's families and soldiers. A high school football team dedicated their season to a unit. They created a unit/team motto of "Seize the Opportunity" and gave the armory a team photo.

170 One deployed mom said that her daughter's guidance counselor formed a "support group" for the students whose parents were deployed.

171 "My daughter organized a school supply drive to stock an Iraqi school that the troops were rebuilding."

Spiritual Protection

There always seems to be controversy that surrounds any reference to spirituality and belief in God. It may be no different here, but it must be said. If this bothers you, feel free to jump past this piece and rejoin us in a few pages.

Over the past two years, in my hundreds of conversations with families, one thing permeates much of what they say about hope. Most of our families hold a firm faith that a "Higher Power" is watching out for their loved one while serving. It is this foundation of belief that allows them to get through each day until they are back together again. It allows them to be able to make explanations to children and help them keep hope alive. It's the subject of many of the songs sung in support of our troops and our love for them.

In this chapter, and other places in the book, you've probably noticed that I offer ideas for how your church communities can be supportive and involved in the lives of the families under God's care. I'm sure there are so many more ways that haven't been shared yet.

172 One thing our church does is to dedicate a bulletin board with pictures, addresses, and messages from our members who are stationed elsewhere. They also post specific needs that the family at home may have so that the church family can go to them directly and know how they can be of assistance. The community prayers during the worship service should always contain a special prayer for the troops.

The military sends our troops off with protective gear for their bodies. Where are they getting the protective gear for their souls? I wholeheartedly support the Chaplain services. They distribute small copies of the entire Bible or the New Testament in pocket form so that they can be carried in the field. That's certainly not all. They also make available copies of the Old Testament/Hebrew Scriptures, the Koran, and the Book of Mormon. When you visit the Chaplain's office and chapel you will find other services such as counseling, worship services for all denominations, unit/squadron visitations, rites, sacraments, and ordinances. All the people I've met around the Chaplains' offices have been wonderful to talk with and are very caring and open. This is a place where you can find the same warmth and comfort you found in the home church community you grew up in.

173 There must be many times when it becomes difficult to believe that God is with you. Try posting the following affirmation on the bathroom mirror:

Remember: God is here to listen and help. Every person I meet today will be in my life for a reason. Have faith for today, and we'll tackle tomorrow when it arrives!

174 I offer this to you, too. It's a prayer of protection that I was given many years ago by someone who cared for me. I carry it all the times I'm away from home. You have my permission to copy it and send it to your serviceperson for him/her to carry with them. Believe me, it helps!

Prayer of Protection

The Light of God surrounds me.
The Love of God enfolds me.
The Power of God protects me.
The Presence of God watches over me.
Wherever I am, God is.

175 This is a wonderful idea that came from a wife at Buckley AFB when I was speaking at the Chaplains Spiritual Fitness Conference in Colorado last year. Each departing serviceperson who would like one is given a brown tee shirt to wear under his/her fatigue's. It's not just any ordinary shirt. It carries with it a tag that says it is "God's Body Armor." (Eph. 6:11) On it are written by hand four additional verses from the Bible that refer to God's protection. The verses cited are: Psa. 144:1-2, Psa. 118:17, Zech. 4:6 and Psa. 68:20. A person volunteered to letter these on both sides of the shirt in a black permanent fabric marker.

176 Our church sent care packages to all our college freshmen twice during their first year. It was just one more way to let the students know that they have a connection to their home and community. What better way for service personnel to feel connected to their community than to have the church send care packages through the appropriate channels. Can you organize something?

177 Here's a tip from a corporate traveler: Rebecca gave her two children Beanie

Babies® positioned in prayer. She told them to put the bears on their pillows and they would know that she was saying a prayer for them from wherever she was. It was so comforting for everyone.

Finally, remember that there are many people around you who can tend to your spiritual needs, questions and concerns. Please don't hesitate to seek them out when you feel you need a little "boost."

"Happy Birthday!" and "Happy Holidays!" – Celebrations Across the Miles

I remember the time I got an email from a woman who wanted to find a way to celebrate her husband's 40th birthday. Not a big problem, except that he was in Iraq! I put her question out to others in my newsletter and received feedback from many on ways to send a "Birthday Party in a Box." This might include balloons, photos of those at home celebrating, Hostess® cupcakes with candles for all the guys in his quarters, presents, homemade cards and music to play during the celebration, and don't forget the disposable camera so you can see the pictures. That started me thinking that assignments often keep families apart for the holidays and celebrations that we're usually together for. It's time to look at a few ways that you can celebrate the special occasions.

178 You've heard of "Christmas in July?" Well one family had Christmas in May...May 9th to be exact. Mom was deploying at the end of May and wouldn't be back for Christmas—her favorite holiday. So the family had a big Christmas celebration *before* she left. They put up and decorated an artificial tree and kept it up until their real Christmas. They had a turkey dinner, played Christmas music and even exchanged presents. She took the photos with her to relive that wonderful day in Afghanistan on December 25th.

179 Margaret shares: "I had a really good idea for my husband's birthday. I went to get my hair done, got a makeover, and had a very special picture made. The theme of the picture is done after the old Vassar Girl posters. I was draped in the USA flag, and beneath was the title 'Freedom is Not Free – Military Wives Know.' I had the picture made in a 20" X 40" poster. Please note that nothing was showing that shouldn't be showing. My husband loved it. He had it hanging in his personal quarters. Afterwards, a friend stated that I should have gathered all the pictures (I had three outfits) into a calendar. Gratefully, he does not have 12 months left so I did not do this, but I would have if I had thought of it sooner. This might be a great idea for other wives."

180 For a birthday, buy small packages of fun snack foods and have the kids wrap each item individually—lots of fun for both sides here. How about a cake? Chocolate frosting in a can and graham crackers seem to travel well. Purchase several birthday cards, one for each child and yourself to mail, and one to pass around at work for everyone to sign. Anyone who walks into the office is asked to sign. Pass another card around at church, as well. Your serviceperson will love them all.

181 For the holiday season, record a favorite family holiday story that can be sent.

182 Trace around family members' handprints and cut them out. Glue them together in a wreath shape and call it "Circle of Love." Each person can sign their own handprint, too.

183 Father's Day—"Using chart-sized lined paper, write a letter using different colored pencils for each family member who contributes. I folded it to letter size and mailed it to the Chaplain. He gave it to my husband on Father's Day and took a picture of him opening his letter. We also included photos and stickers, which gave him something to hang on his wall."

184 "In keeping with tradition, we always have birthday parties. When my husband was deployed our entire extended family got together for his birthday. I had him call home to be a part of his party and we could sing Happy Birthday right to him. We videotaped the party and we had all his favorite party foods. Everyone brought cards for him—58 in all! The cards and tape were sent to him."

185 Anniversary—"Take a large Teddy Bear (or one of your children's favorite stuffed animals) with you as a 'spouse stand-in' (or use a *Flat Daddy* figure) for a nice dinner out with the children. Have the waitress take a photo of all of you, including the stuffed animal. When you mail the photo, also send the receipt showing where you went and a paper menu with what you ate circled. If there was a kid's placemat, mail that as well."

186 I love this poem written by a friend of mine to accompany a gift on Valentine's Day.

Even though we're miles apart,
you're with me always in my heart.
Freedom for you I will pray.
May God be with you every day.

Chapter 3

About Family Services Centers
Use your support group as a safety net.

There are many unique demands imposed on a military family during the course of a military career. These range from frequent relocations and separations, to living with the threat and risk of injury or death. These demands can make it more difficult to fulfill both work and family commitments. This has been particularly hard since the events of September 11, 2001, and the increased activation of Reserve troops. As of October 5, 2005, the total number of National Guard and Reserve personnel (from all branches) who have been mobilized for the war on terror are 142,614, including both units and individual augmentees.[4]

Following the abolition of the draft in 1973, the government saw the need for coordinating the military and family lives of its members. This was due to a shift from two-thirds single personnel to almost two-thirds married personnel.[5] Family Service and Support

Centers started to emerge to smooth the conflicting demands of the military lifestyle.

By 1993, an annual congressional appropriation of $137 million funded a worldwide network of 370 Family Centers with a combined staff of 3,150 human services professionals. Despite the impacts of downsizing, as of October 2005, the DoD (Department of Defense) retains 284 Family Centers around the world for 670,000 service members and 1.3 million of their children.[6]

I'm Already Home and *I'm Already Home...Again* were made possible with the care and cooperation of representatives and volunteers from military Family Readiness Centers. All branches of the service have a form of this center available to service personnel. They may be called Family Services, Family Readiness, Family Support Centers, or programs under the Chaplain's Office. They describe themselves as "families helping families," and they all do their part to ensure that military members and their families experience the highest possible quality of life.

During the past two years I've visited with many volunteers from Family Support Centers of all different kinds. Some centers were small, some were quite extensive. Some unit programs were run from the volunteer's home and others out of a local armory or on base or post. These centers were similar to the families they served: they might look different on the surface but have a strong underlying strength. The purpose of bringing you this section is to share ways that families have used the services that support facilities provide, as well as some of what they have gleaned from the support of other families.

Military leaders learn early that "if you take care of the people, the people take care of the mission."[7] These Centers use peacetime to build strength, trust, and resources so that they are able to be most effective during activation. Each state operates units and groups that are a vital part of a larger program that continues all the way to the Pentagon.

The military family is also part of a larger family—their military community. The Family Readiness Group establishes a link with this community to help promote awareness. Communication is a major goal for the unit volunteers. They get involved with tasks like developing a telephone tree as a quick system for passing messages to Guard and family members. Other lines of communication can include unit newsletters, questionnaires, volunteer coordination, and an annual conference. To help increase social integration, they network with other local and off-base organizations and civic groups. Maintaining these relationships provides open contact and awareness of the Centers' programs and their professional counterparts. This results in less duplication of services and more collaboration.

Family Readiness Centers are a vital part of helping families get ready for deployment. They can help a family plan ahead and take care of legal, medical, financial, and personal issues. Specifically, a military family can work with their Readiness Center for assistance with referrals and questions. These questions can fall into, but not be limited to, the following issues:

- Personal property
- Estate planning
- Wills and guardianship
- Powers of attorney
- Family problems or difficulties
- Mail
- Benefits and assistance
- Insurance
- Housing and relocation
- Military installation facilities
- Chaplain support
- Alcohol and drug abuse prevention programs
- Spouse employment aid
- Mobilization
- Transition to civilian career
- Family life skills education

You may not be aware of how vital the Family Readiness Centers are. Guidance and support are offered to extended family members (parents, grandparents, etc.) of service men and women. Members of the community sometimes get involved, as well. Many companies or corporations sponsor Reserve units by sending mail and/or gifts, and doing nice things for the service members' families who remain behind.

Now here's the fun part. I get to share some of the wonderful things that units and support centers are doing for the servicepersons and their families. Maybe you can take an idea or two back to your own

FRC and put it into action there. Remember, all projects had to start with the seed of an idea from someone. Be that someone.

187 Let's start with a superb idea from Don Miller, Family Assistance Center Coordinator: "Shortly after a unit from Nebraska deployed we had everyone who was missing their soldier get into the dresser and find an old uniform t-shirt (preferred) or a favorite t-shirt belonging to him/her. We put in name tags and sent them to the soldiers overseas and requested they wear them for a few hours (no PT) and then send them back unwashed. We then sewed the neck and arms shut, stuffed them like a pillow and sewed the bottom shut. You would be surprised the effect the pillows had on the family members. Even after the unit had been home for months the pillow subject comes up and we learn how, when someone is feeling low, a big squeeze of the pillow picks up the mood."

188 "We bought some sheets of lightweight balsa wood (1/4") and during a family unit meeting had each person trace their hand on the piece of wood. Then the adults cut them out with craft knives. Each person signed and dated their hand, punched a small hole near the edge with an awl, and we strung them together on a length of yarn like a chain. We displayed this chain in the squadron."

189 "I'm the key volunteer for my families and I often receive information about what the airmen are doing while on assignment. I love to do scrap booking, so when I learn new information I make a card for the family and include a personalized note referencing the airman by name, a project/task he or she is working on, and a note of encouragement for the family member. Nothing we do to recognize our airmen is generic; it's all as personal as we can be. The effect on the family is so much nicer."

190 "We have each family bring in the children to the armory and take recent photos of each child individually. Check out your unit members for someone who has the equipment—and talent—to take good pictures. Have copies of these pictures made and give them to each child who then glues them to the front of their very own note cards."

191 A unit had pictures taken of each soldier with their kids or significant other at the armory. The soldier was dressed in uniform against an all black background. So these photos were beautiful and a bit more formal. Embossed on it is the soldier's name, email address, and *"Thank you for your prayers."* Some families had wallet size copies made to give out to those who would like to send a note.

192 One group did a banner at a FSG meeting. The kids dipped their hands in paint and then put handprints on the banner. Everyone there wrote a message, too. It was then rolled and mailed to the unit.

193 I pulled the following from an email I received because it was so touching. Many times we don't realize how the families are utilizing even the smallest resources we can set up. "I really feel connected through the Navy News Site, the John C. Stennis website, and any other online resources I can find. Seeing pictures of what the crew of the Stennis is doing helps me know where my son is and what he is doing. I'm sure that other branches of the service have the same resources. When he was in port in San Diego there was a webcam set up that overlooked the Naval Station. My husband and I both would watch his ship leave port and return, and it made us feel that we were watching him. Because of the distance between us (Wisconsin and California) it was amazing to feel so close. He even called us one day and told us to watch because he was going up on deck. We saw him and he waved to us and blew us a kiss. Awesome, huh?"

194 The guys in Iraq have a "battle buddy." Along these lines, Deb's group has set up a "Buddy-up" list. It's vaguely similar to a phone tree. She took the roster of wives, put her name on the bottom, and distributed the list. Once a week you are asked to call and touch base with the person on the list directly above you. It's totally random. Maybe you can have lunch...maybe just ask how they're doing. What makes this program so good is that it's set up with others who are in your shoes. They know what you're going through and that can make a great deal of difference.

Family Service Centers ultimately show us that we ALL have a stake in our military families. The members of the armed forces are out there for us, and we should be a supportive part of bringing them back to a stable and happy family environment.

The only thing we've found
that makes the emptiness bearable
is each other.

—from the movie Contact

Chapter 4

Post-deployment...and Beyond

Reunion and Reintegration

The good news is...your spouse is coming home! The bad news is...your spouse is coming home! Getting back on track might not be as easy as it sounds.

This is the one area where I found that the most changes have occurred over the past two years since the writing of the first book. Reunion and reintegration has started to take center stage in the life of a deployment. And so has redeployment. At first, families would "stick it out" thinking that it's only going to be this one time. That's been a rude awakening. Going through two or three deployments is becoming more and more common. Even through the unknowns, the families I've met have stepped up to the challenge and continued to work harder and stronger to keep this from taking a permanent toll on their family. What do they say helps them the most? Being "proactive" instead of "reactive." They know more now about what it's going to be like, and they know where to go for information. They know they have to take charge of their own lives and create the best environment they can for those around them. One woman specifically told me that things really did change when she stopped feeling sorry for herself and started making memories for her family!

Something else that happened since 2003 has been the overwhelming amount of information I've accumulated from myriad sources pertaining to this post-deployment phase. While it's great to know more so that I can help more, I approach this section feeling like I just have to share everything with you! Now we all know that's not only impossible, it's inappropriate. I had to keep telling myself that I'm not a psychologist, but I am a person who's had the privilege of talking with hundreds of people who have been going through this. My job is to share the things that these real families have done to make reunion easier, and that's what I will spend most of these pages doing. Just because I'm not a counselor doesn't mean that I can't bring you advice from one or two. I'll be doing that, too.

I found many good resources to help with challenges like Post Traumatic Stress Disorder (PTSD), reunion advice for families and communities, deployment cycle support, and transition for active duty service to civilian life. Rather than provide synopses of these programs, I've listed many of them in the "Resources and Support" section of the book. One booklet that I really did like is called *"Reintegration: Beyond Reunion – A guide for service members and their families."* Ask your support office if they have a copy for you. If not, you can order them by calling toll free 1-800-628-7733, or visiting www.channing-bete.com, and asking for item number PS92753.

Here's something fun and interesting to begin with. Often during the breakout sessions at family readiness conferences, we ask the spouses in attendance, "What is something you're concerned about with your spouse coming home?" The responses are always wonderful. Here is a countdown of the six most common responses:

6. Living together again and feeling nervous and uncertain about it.

5. Getting him/her into the routine again with the children's activities; i.e., sports, homework, school, and social events.

4. Getting used to becoming independent, and having your husband coming back and taking over.

3. Having another adult in the house.

2. Discipline—the children are not accustomed to Dad being "the boss" again.

and my all time favorite...

1. Coping with snoring!

Hopefully we'll find ideas or advice to help with as many of these concerns as we can. Although I don't know about the snoring.

It All Starts at the Airport

The schedule for returning home starts at the airport and the first ride home. It seems like a good place to start with the next four contributions.

195 When meeting your serviceperson's plane, have a really large poster board with their name on it so they can spot you...because the soldiers "all look alike in uniform!" Decorate the poster with your own flair.

196 Have the unit create a welcome home banner with ALL the soldiers' names on it and make another one with the names of the fallen soldiers. This is a recognition that often passes us by at the return home.

197 This is called "Every Step You Take, I'll Be Watching You." Find places to post signs along your loved-one's route from the airport (or base) to home. Some examples of signs to make and hang are "30 miles to Love"..."20 miles to home cooking" "10 miles to the remote"..."2 miles to hugs", etc. You'll think of some great ones.

198 When pulling in the driveway, he will see 100 yellow ribbons tied to the trees in front of the house, and perhaps he'll hear the yellow ribbon song, too!

Ready for the next step? Sounds like there might be a homecoming party in the wings. But first, it's important not to go overboard immediately. Many families tell me that it's really hard to hold back. The first key is to discuss the plans you're considering for homecoming with the person who will be returning. Ask them what they have in mind, if anything. Do they want a party right away, or would they rather have a week or so to unwind and then have a party? You'll want to know this. This holds true for all absences and returns, no matter the length or purpose. At the very least, it's the courteous thing to do, and this communication can avoid a disruption of how you envisioned the activities. Here's what some families have done:

199 "We had a small welcome home with just my returning wife, me and the kids. I actually made a great dinner and just let her sit back and enjoy. Then we waited about two or three weeks and had a big outside barbeque with our parents and friends. She was so grateful that she didn't have to have lot's of people around right away." Something to consider.

200 "We called our welcome home party *My Favorite Things.* They were all there—all his favorite things that he missed while gone like favorite foods, favorite dessert, decorations in favorite colors, favorite pictures, a video of events, and of course favorite friends. While everyone was together, we showed the video our family made. We called it *Video of the Year Missed.*"

201 "My husband was gone on assignment for six months and when he got back we included everyone in a welcome back block party in the neighborhood. It was easier to invite people to a party like that, and I had lots of help from the neighbors preparing things like salads. We set up grills in the street and it was really informal. Then my husband could feel free to 'hang back' and recollect as he wanted to."

202 Here's something fun. "We used *Time Magazine's Person of the Year* cover (the one that honors the American Serviceperson) and placed my daughter's face on the face of one of the soldiers and screened it onto t-shirts for the entire family."

203 One mom kept a copy of all the emails, with the replies, that were exchanged with her son during his assignment. She printed them all, 3-hole punched them, and put together a notebook. When he returned, she gave him this notebook at the homecoming party. Afterwards, as he was readjusting, he loved rereading these because it let him remember all that he had done on assignment to help others. You tend to forget the impact you can have.

Fitting Back in Again

This part's for the returning serviceperson. Things happened while you were gone, as they had to in order for your home to continue to run itself. Responsibilities changed and sometimes people had to change, too, in order to meet the needs of the household.

The spouse who remained home discovered that he/she really could balance the checkbook, call in repairmen, do the cooking, get all the kids to where they had to go and when, and make the available money last for the expected length of time. Those successes make people feel good about who they are and what they can accomplish when the need arises; however, feelings of inadequacy may develop if it didn't go as well as planned.

You're home now, so everything can return to *normal*—whatever that is—but probably not right away. There will be a transition period where you'll become "reacquainted" again as a family. Take time to observe your children in their everyday routines, and slowly allow yourself to become a part of those routines again.

You'll need to reacquaint yourself again with your spouse, too. Talk about how everything got done at home in your absence. See what worked and what didn't. Maybe things don't have to go right back to the way they were; it might not be the best solution. The key is to share your expectations with each other. Ask your spouse, *"Do you want to hand over the checkbook right away, or did you find that you enjoyed that responsibility?"* Perhaps he/she would like to continue to be an active part of your family's financial planning.

Don't keep all your thoughts secret, but do allow for some "welcome home" time to pass as you bask in the rediscovery of each other. We'll start with a few ideas designed to help you begin the reconnection process.

Here's a tip from a family counselor: Remember the importance of maintaining closeness and intimacy during the absence, as well as when you're together. Then it will feel just like the continuation of what you've been building all along. She also shared, "Love is a decision; decide on romance."

204 How about starting with 1001 ideas! Get a copy of *1001 Ways to be Romantic* by Gregory Godek. You'll find it at most bookstores or on www.Amazon.com. From simple ideas like writing "I love you" on the bathroom mirror with a piece of soap, to filling your lover's car with balloons, to more *steamy* ideas when you're ready—it will help turn your marriage back into a love affair!

205 Here's an amazingly simple and fun way to spend a little time together. If you have children, you can include them if you'd like. "When my husband came home, we went to one new place a day. Some were new businesses or someplace I found while he was gone." The best part is experiencing these together.

Along these same lines my husband, Larry, and I planned a driving vacation. We had an "ending point" which was to arrive in Michigan on a certain date to attend my niece's graduation. We had two weeks to get there. The design of the entire trip was that everything we did and every place we ate and stayed was someplace we had never been before. So in South Dakota we saw the National Woodworkers Museum (who knew?) and toured that. We saw Mt. Rushmore, and took a train for the first time to the Mall of America (nope, never been there) in Minnesota. It was not only fun to see and do new things, but great that we were seeing and doing them for the first time together. Maybe this would be a nice way to pretend that things are new and wonderful for you, too.

206 After about two or three months following the return home, the two of you need to get away for a weekend to a nice resort or location that has each of your favorite activities (like golf, shopping, touring, etc.). It's vital to reconnect on your own, but also important that you don't jump right into this immediately. If you allow two to three months, you'll find that you're more comfortable with each other and might feel less guilt about leaving the kids again right away. Can't afford a "getaway weekend?" I know that many Chaplain services are sponsoring these weekends as they can. Ask of other programs available, too, like dinner cruises. I know they're out there.

207 Let's start reconnecting with the rest of the family with a "My Daddy (Mommy) Box."

Take a box (like a shoebox) and let your child decorate the outside. Then he/she fills it with anything they want to show the returning parent. For example, school papers, pictures, thoughts, awards, etc. Then when the parent returns, they make their special time to sit down and go through the box. Each child does his/her own so they are truly personal.

208 Create a book of coupons for redemption upon your return. Some suggestions: For kids—movie with Mom or Dad, candy bar of your choice, Dairy Queen® trip, making their favorite dinner, or out to their favorite restaurant. For spouse—time together, hugs and kisses (or more), favorite romantic dinner, doing one of the spouse's chores around the house, etc.

209 Start now to create a book of entries entitled "The most important thing I learned today." Compile these lessons and give the *book of knowledge* to your child upon graduation from high school. It will always go with him/her as a foundation for whatever avenue he/she chooses to take.

210 Share time with your school age children. Discuss some of what it was like to be deployed. Be an integral part of what's going on in their lives. Write notes of encouragement for a project or activity they're doing in school. Put the notes in their lunch boxes or on their pillows at night. Start with shorter notes for younger children and then you can get more involved as they grow older.

211 Have a special "date" between each parent and each child. This is his or her own personal time alone with that parent. Maybe go to dinner and a movie, or a museum, the zoo, shopping, children's concert, or other individual interest. The "dates" that my dad and I had were when I spent hours working with just him while he edited our 8mm home movies. I was the one who narrated them on the sound stripping, and I helped him create titles for the segments. He went all out with our movies—and I was a big part of it; but best of all was that it was *our time* together. One of my friends had *Date Night* with her dad, too. Their favorite activity was going to play miniature golf and then off to Dairy Queen® for an ice cream cone dipped in chocolate!

212 Here's a short summary checklist of things to be aware of:

- Feelings of anxiety and nervousness are normal...for everyone. You might wonder, "Will they still need me and love me?...be proud of me?"

- The days around homecoming can be stressful. Plan reunion activities together so that everyone's needs can be balanced.

- Get back into regular routines slowly...and communicate! Depend on each other for your support.

And now some words of advice about PTSD from a counselor. Linda has been married to a National Guardsman for 34 years. Just completing a three-year term as the State Lead Volunteer, she is the lead instructor for the CISM sponsored Trained Crisis Responder course in North Dakota. You might want to bookmark this page for reference often. Here's what Linda's experience can bring to you:

Reunion: Prospect and Possibility
by Linda Engelman

As you look to reunion you probably hope that life will soon return to normal. You have been told that weathering a lengthy, dangerous deployment will change you, creating a "new" normal. But many of you have no previous experience on which to predict your responses. Therefore, with the anticipation can come some uneasiness.

Because knowledge eases anxieties and helps put things in perspective, I've been invited to provide some information about reunion and Post-traumatic Stress.

It is not only common for military members to experience Post-traumatic Stress, it is expected. A normal response to an abnormal situation, reunion is a time of re-adjustment, a time of transition—literally from one world to another—for your military member.

For family members it is a time for reintegration, a time for opening the family boundaries to make room for the returning veteran. This is both exciting and stressful for everyone. So while I will focus specifically on the military member, know that the whole family can be at risk.

What are some common PTS responses?

Military members often report the following.

1. Feeling flat, apathetic and lethargic. Living under constant threat (and with all the other irritants) results in high levels of hormone (like adrenaline) production. Coming home, as adrenaline levels go down, the lack of stimulation can result in depression.

2. Feeling isolated and lonely. One young soldier said that in Iraq, if she had a problem or concern, there was always somebody to talk with. Now there isn't that constant availability.

3. Feeling guilty. "I should be in Iraq helping," or "Why did I survive and my buddy die?"

4. Feeling on edge. Called the hyper-startle reflex, it takes a while to quit looking for an M16, to quit flinching at sudden sounds, to relax when noticing debris by the road, etc.

5. Feeling like they don't fit-in and experiencing grief over the losses, including missing their military family in Iraq. Families report finding their military member staring out the window for long periods or going for car rides alone. Following such a dramatic and life-altering experience, it takes time to completely come home.

6. Additionally, common responses include:
   - Difficulty concentrating
   - Preoccupation with the event
   - Anxiety, mood swings, headaches
   - Anger, fear, phobic avoidance
   - Loss of appetite and/or energy
   - Sleeping too much or too little
   - Self-medication, often with alcohol

- Withdrawal from church or anger at God
- Family discord, arguing, crying
- Reoccurring dreams
- Risk-taking behavior

When should we think about talking with a professional?

While it is common for symptoms to appear at any time, frequently they start three to six months after returning—when the honeymoon period is over.

Always consult a professional if symptoms don't diminish significantly within 30 days. And, always consult a professional if symptoms are dangerous or debilitating.

Finding a therapeutic listener can insure that this experience is integrated into the fabric of your life, rather than defining your whole life. Looking to the veterans of previous wars, we know that folks can live well, having long, fulfilling, productive lives. Doing the right things today can make ALL the difference!

How can I find a professional?

There are a number of ways to access help:

1. Call your Family Assistance Center or Family Program Office for a referral. Be sure and ask about the free counseling sessions available through One Source to veterans and their families.
2. Call your family physician.
3. Ask your military chaplain or civilian minister.
4. Go to your local Veterans Center.

If the first person you talk to isn't helpful, don't give up! Be persistent and try another. As in other traumatic times, it is not advisable to make major life-changing decisions for at least a year. In the end, this experience can strengthen you and add depth and substance to your life. It is full of prospect and possibility!

[You can read more about Linda in the "Permissions" section at the back of this book.]

In a casual conversation we had, Linda told me that the key piece of advice she would offer is not to make **major** decisions in the first six months of returning home, whenever possible. Don't buy a new house or car, change jobs, or file for divorce. Too much readjustment occurs during these six months, and you may very well settle in and feel differently about the decision after that time.

Returning to Single Life

Much of this book is geared to the "married with children" military demographic. I realize that many of those serving in the military are single. I'll take a few moments to share some thoughts that have been expressed to me concerning the return to single life following assignment or deployment. Most of the advice I heard was very similar to that for families, but a few differences did stand out.

The first is the support system that's in place for you upon return. Having parents, siblings and friends there for you is wonderful but can feel different from having a spouse and kids. That's ok, but you may find it harder to relate to your friends and relatives. More than likely, you may not have stayed connected with them with the frequency that you had hoped. So if you all feel a bit awkward at first, keep making the effort and you should fall back in step with each other soon. Remember, they probably feel awkward, too.

Friends and extended family can't know as intimately as you what you have been through. Try to take some time to relate experiences in a more casual setting, and be patient with them. Help them to understand and be respectful of each other's feelings. Realize, too, that their circumstances may have changed. Some friends may have moved on from jobs or even out of the community. Life went on for them and now yours has to, as well.

First, get your housing situated so that you begin to feel yourself reestablishing roots. Then you can begin to get other areas of your life back in order. Once you know where you'll be living, you can reevaluate your career goals based on your interests and financial needs. Maybe you'll be staying where you are, or maybe this is the time to make a change since you're a bit freer of relationship commitments. Looking ahead at where you can go with the support of friends and associates around you can be an exciting time of new beginnings.

To close this section, it's my pleasure to share part of an email I received from Tim, in the Navy who is frequently sent out on six-month assignments. He gave me permission to share his thoughts and it's the perfect "smile" we need here.

"Now let me let you in on my version of David Letterman's Number 1. Drum roll please! The Number 1 thing about a six month deployment is when the ship pulls back into port and I see the faces of my wife and daughters. There is no room for being too proud to be a man...the tears just roll. That first hug and kiss after six months! There is nothing to compare. The pain, agony, negative emotions, and worrying ALL disappear in one moment as I sweep all three of them up in my arms. That's what makes it worth it and that's what gets you through it."

The two pieces of advice that summarize this chapter seem to be:

Go Slowly.
Put trust in those around you.

Epilogue

It's been a wonderful journey sharing the ways that families around the world have learned the joy of staying connected.

I'm closing this book with one of the most appropriate emails I have ever received. I believe that it sums up most of what we've been talking about all along. It touched me so much that I have it hanging on the wall in my office. It was a reply to me from my son who is 600 miles away at college, following an email I sent to him advising him of a safety alert for college campuses. Here's what he sent back, and I trust that he won't mind if I share it with you.

> *Hey Mom, I just wanted to say thank you for that little bit of advice. I will also make sure to tell some of the other people around here. I had no idea that this was a problem. I would have definitely been one to pull over right away for a car with sirens. Thanks for always looking out for me. I know I may get embarrassed sometimes or even upset because you do it so much, but don't listen to me or ever pay attention to that. You always seem to find some way to help me out and I am grateful. You always know what to do. Thanks for looking out for me and loving me as much as you do. Have a wonderful day and I love you. Tell Dad the same for me, please. Talk to you soon. Bryan*

I love you, too, Bryan. Goodnight.

Resources and Support

www.nmfa.org
National Military Family Association, Inc.
Email: families@nmfa.org
The only private national organization designed to identify and resolve issues of concern for military families. Serves all uniformed services.

www.redcross.org
American Red Cross

www.redcross.org/services/afes/
American Red Cross Armed Forces
Emergency Services

www.operationuplink.org
Donate a calling card through Operation Uplink.

http://www.OperationDearAbby.net
Email greetings through Operation Dear Abby.

http://www.defendamerica.mil/nmam/html
Sign a virtual thank you card to military members.

www.treatsfortroops.com
Also home of Foster-A-Soldier™ Program. Send a gift of your choice from the Treats For Troops Gift Shop. Your gift will be packed and shipped according to all USPS and military regulations. Very easy and fun to do.

http://deploymenthealthlibrary.fhp.osd.mil/home.jsp
This library provides service members, families, veterans and healthcare providers an easy way to quickly find deployment health and family readiness information. Site includes fact sheets, guides, products, and links to organizations and resources devoted to your health and welfare.

http://www.cinchouse.com
A nonprofit organization and the Internet's largest community of military wives and women in uniform. Also the home of a wonderful book, "Married to the Military" by Meredith Leyva.

www.heartsacrossthemiles.org
An all volunteer, nonprofit organization that ensures U.S. troops are not forgotten by providing letters of support, calling cards, and care packages. Also provides support to the families left behind.

Official Military Websites:

www.army.mil
Army

www.army.mil/usar
Army Reserve

www.af.mil
Air Force

www.afrc.af.mil
Air Force Reserve

www.usmc.mil
Marine Corps

www.marforres.usmc.mil
Marine Force Reserve

www.arng.army.mil
Army National Guard

www.ang.af.mil
Air Force National Guard

www.navy.mil
Navy

www.navalreserve.com
Naval Reserve Force

www.uscg.mil
Coast Guard

www.uscg.mil/hq/reserve/reshmpg.html
Coast Guard Reserve

www.va.gov
Veterans Affairs

Military relief societies:

http://www.aerhq.org
Army Emergency Relief

http://www.nmcrs.org
Navy/Marine

http://www.afas.org
Air Force Aid Society

http://www.specialops.org/contribute.html
Special Operations Warrior Foundation

http://www.taps.org
Tragedy Assistance Program for Survivors

http://www.ustreas.gov
Purchase a Patriot Bond

www.sgtmoms.com
Sgt. Mom's is "Military Life explained by a
Military Wife!"
It is not an official DoD site or related to any official
organization. It's a fun site filled with relevant
information and links presented in a clear, navigable
way.

www.deploymentlink.osd.mil
DeploymentLINK is maintained by the Office of the
Special Assistant to the Under Secretary of Defense for
medical readiness and deployments. It links to National
Guard and Reserve web sites.

www.read2kids.org/uniting.htm
The Family Literacy Foundation provides a program for
military families to help keep parents and children
connected during deployment through reading aloud on
videotapes.

www.abanet.org/family/military/checklist.pdf
A volunteer lawyers group has prepared an excellent
Family Member Pre-Deployment Checklist. It is
designed for all families and includes record-keeping
questions related to medical care, finances, etc.

www.armycommunityservice.org/home.asp
Army Community Service provides real-life solutions
for successful Army living.

www.defenselink.mil/ra/familyreadiness.html
Resources such as the Family Readiness Tool Kit and
Guide to Reserve Family Member Benefits Handbook
in PDF format are available on this site.

www.DivorceNet.com
Military divorce, family law, and counseling. Source of
articles and information.

www.4MilitaryFamilies.com
Support groups, discounts, travel, housing, and
deployment information.

www.mfri.purdue.edu
Military Family Institute is a DoD sponsored research
center with a focus on families.

http://www.dfas.mil/money/garnish/supp-qa.htm
Defense Finance and Accounting Service answers some
FAQ's about child support issues.

www.Groww.com
GROWW is an independent haven for the bereaved
developed by the bereaved. Message boards and resource
listings.

http://Militarywivesandmoms.org/godblessusa.html
A site designed for those who have husbands, sons, or
daughters proudly serving our country in the armed
forces.

www.Military.com
Connecting you to the benefits of service. It's an amazing
site filled with information pertaining to all branches of
services. It's always kept current.

http://www.bluestarmothers.org
Designed for mothers who have, or have had children serving in the military. Good information easily arranged.

http://www.thestandinthegapproject.org
Providing financial assistance and outsourcing to help Colorado families and Colorado troops.

http://www.geocities.com/mydaddyfightsforfreedom
Gives children a realistic outlook about their parents' deployment and tools to help deal with their feelings.

http://www.trianglearc.org/afes/treasuresfor troops.htm
A year-round program to brighten the day for deployed men and women by providing a gift from home for a $20 donation specifically to the Treasures for Troops.

http//:www.commissaries.com/certificheck/index.htm
The Gift of Groceries program helps meet the needs of Guard and Reserve families.

http://www.aafes.com/docs/homefront.htm
"Gifts from the Homefront" certificates from the Army Air Force Exchange System. Send these to a love one associated with the military. They are redeemable worldwide by authorized patrons of the PX/BX.

http://www.defendamerica.mil/nmam.html
Sign a virtual thank you card.

www.freedomteamsalute.army.mil
Nominate a military support person (spouse, employer, etc.) for recognition and award for all they do! Great idea.

http:www.militaryhomefront.dod.mil
Through sponsorships, military family children can receive SAT/ACT Standard Power Prep programs at no charge.

Additional Sources for Reunion and Reintegration:

www.channing-bete.com
You'll find information to order the booklet "Reintegration: Beyond Reunion – A guide for service members and their families." Or call 1-800-628-7733 and ask for item number PS92753.

www.militaryonecource.com
A 24-hour, 7 day-a-week counseling service available to anyone who has been deployed or affected by a loved one's deployment. There are many other opportunities available on the site, too. You can also call toll-free 1-800-342-9647.

http://www.usmc-mccs.org/MCFTB/return.asp
Return and Reunion guide, information, and brief. Operation Iraqi Freedom Warrior Transition

http://www.nmha.org/reassurance/
MentalHealthWarMilitaryFamilies.cfm
The National Mental Health Association: *Coping with War-related Stress: Information for Military families and communities*

http://www.deploymentguide.com
Deployment Guide 2003 includes Readjusting after a Deployment

http://www.ncptsd.org/
The National Center for Post-Traumatic Stress Disorder:
Iraq War Clinician's Guide

www.usuhs.mil
Center for the Study of Traumatic Stress as an ongoing
source of information and support

http://www.nmha.org/reunions/index.cfm
Article titled *Operation Healthy Reunions.* It's a well
written, informative and upbeat article that covers
many areas of reunions.

Resources for Veterans of Operation Iraqi Freedom and Operation Enduring Freedom:

http://www.vba.va.gov/
Veterans benefits information

http://www.va.gov/gulfwar/
Information for Iraqi Freedom Veterans

http://www.va.gov/environagents/
Afghanistan service information

http://www.ncptsd.org/topics/war/html
PTSD and Iraq veterans

http://www.va.gov/elig/
VA health care enrollment information

http://www.vethealth.cio.med.va.gov/Pubs/Index.htm
Brochures and publications including a summary of
VA benefits for National Guard and Reserve Personnel,
and healthcare and assistance for U.S. Veterans of
Operation Iraqi Freedom

http://vabenefits.vba.va.gov/vonapp/
Online benefits applications

http://www.va.gov/wvhp/
http://www.va.gov/womenvet/
http://www.vba.va.gov/bln/21/Topics/Women/
Women veterans health and benefits information

Volunteer Opportunities:

Are you finding yourself a little lonely with some extra time on your hands? Consider volunteering for a worthwhile organization based on your interests. Here are a few sites to start with:

www.adoptaclassroom.org
Connects the community and the classroom. Contribute to the education of young people.

www.beadsforlife.com
Make bead key chains and necklaces that call attention to early detection of breast cancer.

www.Chemocaps.com
This site is for knitters. Donate your time by knitting caps for cancer patients. Comfort their heads and their souls.

http://h4ha.org/snuggles
Hugs for Homeless Animals is a site designed to wrap animals with love by sewing or knitting warm blankets for them.

www.Projectlinus.org/index.html
Provides love, security, warmth, and comfort to children who are seriously ill or traumatized, through gifts of new/homemade washable blankets.

http://www.wtv-one.com/kjsb/bataan.html
The Ships Project Supports American troops at sea and on the ground in Operation Enduring Freedom. Crochet, knit or quilt.

Volunteer at a VA Hospital to honor veterans who fought for freedom throughout time.

In Appreciation

While I received hundreds of family connection ideas to share, the following people gave me permission to put a name with their thoughts. Many thanks to all the families who contributed their ideas, and their hearts, to make better families. This project *is* you!

Angel Hernandez

Bev Day

Billie Ivey

Brad Montgomery

Carl Carlson

Carolyn Foster

Cathy Hammock

Christine

Christine Collins

Cindy Bruschwein

Craig Lyons

Darcey Grindel

Darlene

Deanna

Debbie Wilder

Diana Brown

Donna Swaney

Glenna Denison

Heather McElheny

Indy Blaney

Janis Smith

Jeannette

Jennifer Strong
Jeremy VanWyk
Judy St.Clair
Judy Wood
Julie Hayden
Justin Holmes
Kathy Moakler
Kelly Bradley
Kim Clark
Kristin DeGruy
Kristin Krieger
Laura DeHennis
LeAnn Thieman
Leisa Hice
Leslie Gonzalez
Libbi Cox
Linda Dubbs
Linda Edmonds
Linda Verbridge
Lisa White
Lori McDonald
Lori Wentworth
Lynn Heald
Major David and Julie-ann Goldstein
Mark Swenson
Mary Fichtner
Michele Anderson
Molly Waneka
Nicole Effle
Patricia Early-Carter
Paula McLain
Rebecca Cox
Rebecca Lyons
Rita Leavesley

Permissions and Information

Lines from *The Prophet*, by Kahlil Gibran, are quoted with the permission of Alfred A. Knopf, Inc. Copyright 1923 by Kahlil Gibran, renewed 1951 by Administrator C.T.A. of Kahlil Gibran Estate and Mary G. Gibran.

Excerpt from *Daily Word*™ reprinted with permission of Unity®, publisher of *Daily Word.*™

Innocence© by Molly Waneka, reprinted with permission of Molly Waneka.

Photograph with idea #25, used with permission of Marlan Sorenson.

Reunion: Prospect and Possibility article written for Elaine Dumler by Linda Engelman and used with permission. Linda has been married to a National Guardsman for 34 years. Just completing a three-year term as the State Lead Volunteer, she is the lead instructor for the CISM sponsored Trained Crisis Responder course in North Dakota. Linda has presented many times at the national Family Program Workshop. Holding a master's degree in clinical counseling, she has 10 years college level experience in teaching and counseling. Available for public speaking on a variety of topics, Linda can be reached at 701-250-7207 or lengelma@bis.midco.net.

Pets and Deployment article: Dr. Suzanne Hetts is a certified applied animal behaviorist, and with her husband, Dr. Dan Estep, co-owns Animal Behavior Associates, an animal behavior consulting firm in Denver, Colorado. Drs. Hetts and Estep are internationally recognized experts in animal behavior, and the authors of several books, videos and CDs. For more information about your pet's behavior, sign up for their free e-zine at www.AnimalBehaviorAssociates.com.

The beautiful pencil drawings are by Matt Baca from Westminster, Colorado.

Footnotes

1. Article – "Military Families in the Millennium", from the newsletter entitled *Family Focus on...Military Families* (issue FF13), published by the National Council on Military Relations.

2. Article – "What Society can Learn from the U.S. Military's System of Family Support" by Sondra Albano, Ph.D. in *Family Focus*, March 2002.

3. *Soldier Attitudes: Military Deployments,* U.S. Army Medical Research Unit-Europe, Walter Reed Army Institute of Research, U.S. Army Medical Research and Material Command.

4. From *60 Minutes* Newsmagazine report aired on March 16, 2003 on CBS affiliate station KCNC, Denver, Colorado.

5. ibid. footnote 2

6. ibid. footnote 2

7. ibid. footnote 2

About the Author...

Elaine Dumler educates in her own unique way – through speaking. Forming **Frankly Speaking** to work with people who wish to bring a sense of craftsmanship into their business presentations, Elaine has grown her company to include a series of presentation skill training and video coaching workshops which have been used by such organizations as General Electric, Johnson & Johnson, and the U.S. government.

Elaine is a wife and mother whose husband served in the Army National Guard from 1969-1975. As a speaker her clients take her around the globe. Recognizing that the stress of separation is there even when the timeline is relatively short, she was particularly touched by what military families face with sustained absences. Sharing the desire we all have to support our military families, Elaine went back to her roots in communication to create **I'm Already Home** (version one), a book designed to help families discover unique and wonderful ways to stay connected and in constant communication when they are apart. Incorporating methods she used to stay connected to her husband and son along with ideas garnered from over 400 military families throughout the country, Elaine created a wonderful resource for any family facing the stress and anxiety of separation. This new book, **I'm Already Home...Again**, combines the best of the original edition with over 150 new ideas, resources, stories, and expanded chapters on reunion, reintegration, pets and deployments, and how communities, schools, and extended families can help. This new information was gleaned through speaking with hundreds more families these past two years.

Now focusing on bringing her message and methods of family unity to military families throughout the country, Elaine has been featured in the October 2004 issue of *Ladies Home Journal*, invited on TV (including MSNBC and FOXNews) and radio (36 programs) to talk about the importance of keeping family ties stronger than ever and the connection strategies most effective in doing so. She is proud to have been presented with 11 different "Military Challenge Coins," including President George W. Bush's Commander in Chief coin, to honor her work with families.

Committed to helping military families at home and abroad, Dumler has been traveling to military installations and family readiness conferences throughout the country with her reassuring strategies for families with one goal in mind: to make sure that every American deployed or on temporary assignment in the service of their country has the means available to be in the closest contact possible with their loved ones left behind. And *I'm Already Home...Again* is a wonderful resource for all of those families.

Contact Elaine: Elaine@ElaineDumler.com.

Also by Elaine Dumler

♥ …Booklet: 10 Keys to Comfortable Conversation

♥ … Book: Marketing for People NOT in Marketing—
How Everyone Can Build Customer Relationships

♥ … "In the Arms of an Angel"—Story in *Chicken Soup for the Nurse's Soul*

♥ … Short Story: *"Budding Love"—Story in Chicken Soup for the Bride's Soul*

♥ … Book: I'm Already Home—Keeping your family close when you're on TDY *(first edition)*

How to Order

- FAX ORDERS   303-430-7679
- TELEPHONE ORDERS   **Call Toll Free: 1-866-780-0460**
- ONLINE ORDERS   www.ImAlreadyHome.com
- POSTAL ORDERS   Frankly Speaking
                                      6460 W. 98th Court
                                        Westminster, CO 80021

- LOCAL TELEPHONE   303-430-0592

I'm Already Home...Again –
Keeping Your Family Close while on
Assignment or Deployment .... $12.95 ea.

Ask for Information on how to **sponsor books** to military families or Family Readiness Centers.

Ask for Information about **Quantity Discounts starting at 25 books!**

Ask for Information about bringing Elaine in to speak at your conference or briefing.

Company Name _____

Name _____

Address _____

Address 2 _____

City_____ State _____ Zip _____

Telephone (_____) _____

Email _____

SALES TAX
Please add 4% for books shipped to Colorado address.

SHIPPING
$2.50 for the first book and $1.50 for each additional book. Call for lower shipping rates for quantities of books over 5.

Total Payment $ _____

_____ Check# _____ Credit Card:_____Visa _____ MasterCard

Card Number _____ Exp. _____ / _____

Signature _____

CALL TOLL FREE AND ORDER NOW!
1-866-780-0460
You can also order online at www.ImAlreadyHome.com